IN THE NAME OF THE FATHER

CHRONICLE OF FRANCO'S SPAIN
TO TRUMP'S AMERICA

IN THE NAME OF THE FATHER

Chronicle of Franco's Spain to Trump's America

Fernando Operé

*Translated
by Rhonda Dahl Buchanan*

literalpublishing

First edition, 2022
En el nombre del padre: Crónica de la España de Franco a la América de Trump. Spain: Valparaíso Ediciones, 2021.

D.R. © 2024, Fernando Operé
D.R. © 2024, Literal Publishing
      Crestón 343
      Ciudad de México, México, 01900

      5425 Renwick Dr.
      Houston, TX, 77081
      www.literalmagazine.com

ISBN: 978-1-942307-58-7

Impreso en Estados Unidos / Printed in the United States

TABLE OF CONTENTS

TRANSLATOR'S ACKNOWLEDGEMENTS

I would like to express my deepest appreciation to Fernando Operé for his assistance and support during the translation process. Although we've been friends for decades, translating his memoir provided new insights about his life and poetry. I am also very grateful to our editor Rose Mary Salum and the editorial team of Literal Publishing for making this translation available to English readers. I would like to thank the following people who read the draft of the translation and offered valuable feedback: my husband Bob Buchanan, who is always my first reader, mi amiga Aída Batiste, who was born and raised in Madrid, and my friend Mara Maldonado, who spent much time in Spain before and after the Franco regime.

To my parents and grandparents
who suffered in their flesh
the Spanish Civil War

Never ask about the true story.

Reality, as you know, always
lies beyond the facts,
beyond the shadow that words cast.
Like those reflections we made as children
that vanished once our hands created them,
leaving us deceived.

Apart from that,
a story doesn't exist until it's told.
If lived, it was fragments of time we tied together,
if narrated, a brittle branch
covered in crystals we pulled from the ice.

PIEDAD BONNETT. *Los habitados*

The passage of time is an illusion, a horizon that frames a
chronology of wounds.

ANDREA JEFTANOVIC. *Escenario de guerra*

1

Lying on the table before me is the old family album that my mother cherished like a treasure. I glance at the photos in black and white and linger over snapshots of relatives posing together, all of them serious, smartly dressed in a slightly elegant manner. They aren't smiling. In those days no one smiled for the camera. That custom took hold in modern times with our need to express happiness, sincere or not, and show everyone how well things are going for us. I don't know if my parents, grandparents, or aunts and uncles were happy. They lived during years that were very hard for them in so many ways. The Spanish Civil War, which lead to World War II, left a trail of death and destruction that they barely managed to overcome by supporting each other with time-worn faith and visits to the church or to the village, where brothers stayed behind planting melons and raising hope. They are Operés and Santillanas. The first, with roots in Aragón, were farmers who moved south to the dry lands of Madrid, to Villaconejos, a remote village between Chinchón and Aranjuez. My grandfather Mariano left to manage the extensive properties of a landowner who rarely set foot on them and lived in a top floor apartment on the Gran Vía in Madrid. My other grandfather, Antonio, hailed from La Mancha, from the town of Villanueva de los Infantes, a region known for literature and good wine. He traveled to the capital in search of a better life and worked as a cabinet maker. A sense of peace and uncertainty can be detected on their somber faces. They look at the camera, or perhaps they're looking at me who writes their story. I'm the one who interrogates them so I can fill in the many gaps in their biographies, as well as my own. What I have no doubt about is their goodness, something along those lines has been preserved in the oral history of the family. My father's goodness and my grandfather's integrity. My Sevillian grandmother was a different story: nimble, lively, carefree, and spirited. In the photograph, she gives me complicit wink. In another photo, my father wears a uniform. Those were the years of the war that caught him in his prime, when one has dreams, and when Madrid seemed on the verge of becoming a grand metropolis. A city where automobiles would take over horse-drawn cars and carriages, where the telephone would connect us to distant places, and typewriters would replace pen and inkwell.

What brought them together? It makes me wonder about our place in those family ties. Is it love that brings together regions, countries, and beliefs? I pose this question from my house in Virginia, where I arrived some forty years ago, with a blond American woman from the Midwest, to create another unforeseen family, far from the Pyrenees and Chinchón, in the Appalachian Mountains, birthplace of bluegrass and pioneers who set out from the coast to build this splendid nation of astounding contrasts.

I have the feeling my mother still looks at me. She never stopped doing so. My grandmother watches over my compulsive ventures. My father remains silent. Perhaps because he's been gone for such a long time, or because his beliefs were so different from mine. In any case, I write in his name, based in part on his past, which isn't mine, although I try to reclaim it.

I have many years under my belt. I've lived almost thirty years of Franco's dictatorship, twenty-five of the transition to democracy, and twenty of the 21st century. I've been a witness to fundamental periods of contemporary Spain and have observed first-hand the declining North American democracy.

In the album there are photos of weddings and baptisms, Sunday strolls to the area around the university campus, and El Parque del Oeste. There are just a few. Most of the photos were taken at a time when there was something worth smiling about. Soon their lives would become complicated, and death would make an appearance, making the photos even more precious. It occurs to me now that these photos may help me reflect upon a past that's closer than I think.

THE SCRIBE

If my grandparents knew,
if only they could foresee,
returning from the grave,
this anguish forged
in universal turmoil,
would they tear their hair out?

I know they don't speak of me,
even if they did
before my time.

If only my father could,
or perhaps desired,
–his head snowcapped–
return after so long

to dot the i's
of grammatical omissions.

If only I could bring him back,
from his abiding night,
to one of these days
swathed in moss,
to one of these skies
so insanely blue,
to the sea and blistering sand.

Could I be the chosen one?
The one they once dreamed about.
That one for whom they burned the last ship?
The one burdened with
the mission of scribe?

But I am to sit down
at the same table,
grasp the parchment
without tearing it,
foretell the past
and transcribe in Gothic letters
"I am the humblest sinner of sinners,
yet I am the one to write
the incomprehensible chronicle of terror,
and of indomitable beauty.
With reluctance I accept
the impossible mission,
without knowing where, how, or when."

I am one of those chosen
from this tragic century. The torch
passes on to me
and scorches my hands.
I must write the chronicle.
I will be the one, the thousandth,
the weary amanuensis,
the obstinate chronicler.

(From *Alfabeto de ausencias/
Alphabet of Absences*)

2

I'm in Washington, D.C., where my oldest son lives. He's light-hearted and carefree, a veritable whirlwind. He's passionate about cooking, acting, sports, politics, and anything controversial. A good appetite is necessary if you're going to devote yourself with enthusiasm to gastronomy, at least with the passion he expends among pots and pans, spices, and aromas. Today, cooking is an art. Creativity and panache are essential to this concoction of fire, condiments, and sauces. We live in a time when chefs are media super-stars. They appear on TV programs, in magazines, and the news. They attend inaugurations, flaunting a prestigious international reputation that comes with today's age of globalization. Before (and when I say before I mean that indefinite time in which all eras belong, those times I know and those I imagine), women did the cooking, as was expected of them. They also washed clothes and dutifully obliged carnal urges. Back then, those services were rendered without a salary, promotions, medals, or pensions. Women cooked and that was that. Relegated to the kitchen, they found themselves in desperate need of learning how to cook, and so they turned to their mother's recipes or their grandmother's, who in turn had inherited them from other mothers and other grandmothers. They learned the basics with finesse or indifference, and passed them on to their daughters who replicated the traditional recipes to a T. Those were perhaps the only recipes. It's not surprising that this culinary tradition is cherished for its ties to the family legacy, home, and blood. That goes for regional inheritance as well, with dishes prepared from local products and served in venerable establishments.

It's different now. Invention and renovation are what matter. The kitchen has been transformed into an experimental laboratory, inspired by the example of Ferrán Adrià, the chef who launched gastronomy to the firmament of Michelin stars, or to the deepest depths of the dark seas where giant squid and seaweed coexist.

My son became enthusiastic about cooking after following the timid footsteps of his father, but primarily out of hunger and an abundance of creativity. A prototype of his generation, he loves to watch great chefs on cooking shows, and then in the company of a friend equally enthralled by the new wave, try out recipes, always with an element of risk and surprise. Without risks, life would be bland, like soup without salt, or a cocktail without alcohol.

I've come to DC to take care of my grandchildren. My son and his wife wanted to celebrate an anniversary and asked us to look after their kids, a six-year-old boy, and a three-year-old girl. At first, I was concerned. It had been a long time since I put my parenting skills into practice on small children, and grand fatherhood fell into my lap like an opportunity to refresh my skills. To what extent should limits be imposed, at what point should order be levied over the natural disorder of children, and should the voice of authority ever prevail over their natural chaotic impulses?

I have four children and never have I wielded an iron-clad paternal authority over them or laid a hand on them, even in the most trying moments of pure turmoil, after they knocked over a fish tank with gallons of water, shattering it to bits and leaving the helpless little goldfish gasping in vain for air on the rug. Even then I didn't smack them on the rear. Back then (once again that undefined era to which I didn't belong, or did unconsciously), it was understood that corporal punishment was not only an acceptable way to raise children, but a laudatory method. "That's how to make them stronger," they used to say, or "let them learn the hard way." I suppose a good measure of military discipline was baked into that formula when I was a boy. The truth is our beatings varied in harshness, from one moment to the next, according to the level of the committed infraction. Sometimes it wasn't necessary to justify the pedagogical benefit because it was understood that punishment was always enlightening. My grandfather used to scare us by threatening to remove his belt. Then he'd take it off to make the threat seem more real, although he never followed through with it. I remember one summer in Talavera de la Reina, near the Tajo River, where I'd spend summers in my aunt and uncle's house. An enraged father had caught his son bathing in the river without his permission. Overwrought because he'd managed to prevent a tragic accident, or simply out of a keen sense of paternal duty, he punished his son's disobedience by parading him naked through the streets of the town, which at that time was much larger than a town, all the while whipping him on the rear with his belt. What must the people watching have thought about such a display of brutality? Would their remarks be laudatory or critical? "That's the way to teach your children," might've been heard. "Well done, he'll learn to obey now," although the repeated use of that term "obey" inevitably leads to rebellion. My mother responded to our infractions brandishing a slipper in the air and running after us down the long hallway of the house. I'd escape through the window thinking I didn't

23

deserve such a disproportionate punishment. On the other hand, my brother Mariano would endure with stoic discipline the shower of slipper swats administered by my poor mother after our riotous acts had propelled her into a choleric state, although by nature, she was serene and sentimental.

In the school of the Hermanos de la Salle, where they supposedly educated me,– what a misleading expression –, they also punished us physically for something as ridiculous as not remembering the name of a king, or the sailor who spotted land on Christopher Columbus's first expedition. They'd beat us with a wooden ball from a contraption designed to keep time, but used by Brother Ceferino for more menacing tasks, to say the least. So, considering such an upbringing, and the adage you are what you eat, I should've turned out to be an experienced disciplinarian given I'd personally suffered the excessive fits of rage of my educators, at school and at home. But no, it didn't turn out that way, and not for lack of will. I thought about it, weighed it over, and felt there was no reason, no matter how great the offense, for me to put my broad, heavy hand on the tender body of my children. And I never did.

I watch my grandchildren as they play their absurd, nonsensical games, as children's games seem in the eyes of adults. I imagine children think the same thing about our games. For the most part, adults stop playing games, opting instead to drink beer senselessly and laugh at someone's stupid remarks. At times, anger prompts us to scream for no real reason and say harmful and terrible things that only a poisoned heart knows how to say. Or we try to outdo each other, breaking records that only serve to feed dark and sinister egos, which emerge when we haven't learned to contemplate pine trees and boulders on a cloudy afternoon, or the savage landscape on a clear summer morning. There's an indecipherable communication between swifts in flight and the air, between clouds and the craggy mountain peaks, between humble wildflowers and crystalline streams. And between our gaze and our skin, the smell of the rain and the sweet autumn breeze. But we learn so little from that language. Perhaps with time and steadfast contemplation, we may discover those ephemeral secrets.

Is a child's gaze better? Does our gaze become clouded when the desires of greed and comfort surface and launch the quest for fleeting triumphs wrapped in all the material forms that come our way?

It's the overwhelming presence of capitalism. And who am I to criticize it? I tell my friends that I'm a bourgeois who only acquires objects of quality, which happen to last longer. I say it in jest, but maybe that's how I feel. Part of my success in life harkens to my humble origins and my escape from the near poverty that engulfed the family when my father left us at only forty-four years of age. Untreatable elevated levels of cholesterol took him away. An air of bereavement filled the house. An overwhelming sadness penetrated the hallway, seeped into my mother's kitchen, into the olive oil and charcoal, into the pots and wooden spoons, plates, and cupboards, and no one could escape that thick and sorrowful tragic mass that took up residence in the house for years. It rose from my mother's eyes, and like a nocturnal tide, swept over the kitchen, the beds and the blankets, the pencils in their case, and the sandals my father would buy us every summer in the Segarra shoe store.

3

Along with my father went his meager salary that, although measly, was enough for the garbanzos, lentils, and white beans we ate daily, with the monotonous crumbs of white bread. Shortly after his death, we were taken out of school and thrust into the labor force. My sister Lourdes became an apprentice to a secretary when she was sixteen. At fourteen, my brother Mariano was hired as an errand boy for Pelimex, a company that distributed Mexican films. As for me, they had to wait a while longer because my twelve years didn't meet the legal minimum age of fourteen to join the workforce, a requirement set by Spain's Franquist government. The perilous necessities of the family budget forced my mother to tell a white lie when she accompanied me on the interview for my first job. I hadn't yet turned fourteen when I started working forty-eight hours a week for Fabra and Coats, a Scottish-Catalonian textile company. That was the beginning of the most chaotic and surreal string of jobs imaginable. I'll come back later to that act of the drama I had to endure because of my father's sudden departure.

How do you revive what's suspended
in the sea of oblivion?
I scan my seafaring chart
and can't find his green eyes,
wayward sailboats sinking
under the vast somber sky.

There's a moving truck
in the back yard, a school,
a vacant convent.

The afternoon ushers in
this orphan's obsession. Mercurial rain.
Ships without a port,
dawn without a horizon.

Memory succumbs
to fleeting abandon.
Her womb is an empty well
between love and death.

I barely remember
the paltry sliver of childhood,
a round tallowed sun,
the Great Bear shining
on starry nights,
and those jasmine kisses of youth.

Benign tumor of memory,
complicity of naught,
alphabet of absences.

(From *Alfabeto de ausencias/
Alphabet of Absences*)

I endured many phases of employment and numerous challenges. Three or four more companies: SEAT, Margaret Astor, Publienvío, until at last and by pure chance, I received one of many gifts from heaven, or from out of the blue, when one of my guardian angels tapped me on the shoulder and introduced me to teaching, which would become one of my most personal and treasured vocations. I started teaching classes on topics I knew absolutely nothing about. I often entered the classroom like a bullfighter stepping into the ring, ready to be gored before an audience who expected more from me than I had to offer. So many times, my knowledge of the subject matter I was supposed to teach was less than what was expected, but I carried on, perhaps out of an instinct for survival. And I was gored only a few times. I must've had something going for me, charisma, some aspect of my gregarious personality, a broad smile that seems sincere, a certain inclination to preach, I don't know, maybe all that and a bit of luck. The thing is I did it fairly well, but the main point is that I liked it, and I still like being in the classroom, looking into the expectant eyes of students and telling them stories. Isn't that what it's all about? Telling stories, being a storyteller, a narrator. There must be some penchant for teaching in the family given two of my siblings devoted their lives to education in one form or another, as did my cousin Jaime and my two nieces Alicia and Laura.

Thanks to teaching, I was able to return to the university. I earned a doctorate and ended up (again under the watchful eye of a guardian angel) at a marvelous university, the University of Virginia, in the state of Virginia. She was like a mother, opening her doors to me, protecting me, educating, and embracing me. More importantly, I was paid a decent salary that allowed me to become the intellectual bourgeois that I am. Wealthy enough to buy bottles of wine that cost more than fourteen dollars and to relax every summer in some part of the world and enjoy the sun, the beach, the sidewalk cafés, and the pleasures of sightseeing. What's more, that salary let me keep writing, teaching, and working in theater, activities that over the years have become part of my DNA.

4

I've spent a week watching my grandchildren at their home outside Washington, D.C. It's been a special time. My grandchildren's names are Ryder, Lulu, Hudson, Penelope, Austen, Eli Ann, and Devon. My father was called Mariano, my mother Rosario, my grandparents Mariano, Ángela, Rosario, and Antonio, names inscribed in the book of saints. Who came up with those names that have nothing to do with my grandchildren's Hispanic heritage? I watch them, hug them, try to play their games with them, all in English, and I can't help but feel the kind and serene presence of my father, although who knows where his bones and spirit may be. He was an Operé from the highlands of Huesca in Aragón, from a remote town at the foothills of the Pyrenees called Bolea, as if the town had been hurled into the air by a ball of granite and landed on a hill, where it grew beneath the shadow of the collegiate church Santa María la Mayor. The church used to be an ancient Arabic castle or palace that defended the territory of Al-Andalus against invasions from Christian kingdoms.

I look at my grandchildren, and despite their gringo names, I feel the blood of my parents flowing into another continent. I already crossed the sea. I've crossed it so many times, many more than Columbus. I figure I've traversed the Atlantic by plane or ship about one hundred forty times, if not more. I've always lived with one foot in each continent. I'm like a bridge connecting east to west, I come and go from both sides, but not my grandchildren. They're Virginians from the east coast, like Jefferson, Madison, and Monroe, venerated fathers of the nation in this country that had neither kings nor saints but reveres the founders as if they were saints. My grandchildren are Operés who inherited the rustic Operé blood, along with the blood that ties them to many other places. But for me, those original roots are bound to the mighty land, the fields, my father's green eyes and his calm gaze, his sturdy hands, and his hearty laughter when someone greeted him or shared a story. The same way my children and grandchildren laugh. How can you not love such peals of laughter that ascend from the base of the throat and echo to the sea?

My father was not well-off, just the opposite. My greatest frustration, which has become tinged with anxiety, is that I never really talked to him. He died when I was twelve years old. At that age, children don't speak or ask questions. They play and observe things without understanding what they see. They feel hunger, fear, more fear, more hunger, prompted by foreboding omens. They daydream and fantasize. They keep their distance, don't speak or ask questions, and barely respond. Conversations with children are reduced to syllables, a few words, a yes or a no, not much more than that. My gentle father died just when he was beginning to relish his paternal role, make plans for the family, and fulfill his desires as a husband. He left us when some of his earthly dreams were coming true, in December of 1958, shortly before Christmas. I stared at his lifeless body without shedding a tear, without answers to so many questions. Even when I saw him laid out in a Franciscan robe that someone, I never knew who, dressed him in, I didn't know what to ask him. Everything happened as if it never happened, on a cold evening, when I was returning home from watching a double feature at the movies of *101 Dalmatians* and *Bridge over the River Kwai*. As I crossed the yard of mulberry trees behind our house, my sister ran toward me, hugged me, and said, "stop singing – I always sang whenever I left the house or came home – don't sing ever again," and she took me inside where a swarm of neighbors and relatives were praying, whispering, and shedding tears.

I couldn't speak to my father or ask him anything. The dead don't speak, and what would I ask him? Why did you die? What will we do now? Why did you leave us with this contagious sadness that seems to cling to the walls like an ominous plague, all the way down the hall, that same hallway where we played? The questions have accumulated over the years. The older I get, the more questions I have. The basic ones: Who are you? What do you think about life, death, the country, poverty, love, God? They tell me he was deeply religious. I remember him in the church at my school where I was an altar boy. At night, when the bedrooms were silent, he prayed the rosary with my mother while they put order into the chaos we left at the end of the day. He'd rise early, drink a cup of cold coffee my mother had left for him, and eat a slice of bread with butter before leaving for some unknown place, unfamiliar like everything he did outside the house. I don't recall that he had close friends, just my Uncle Felipe, with whom he'd go to soccer matches on Sundays at the old Metropolitano field near our house to watch his team Atlético de Madrid play. I also remember his brother Ignacio, who chose to remain in the village growing melons and acres of olive trees and corn. My father didn't stop by the bar before coming home like other men of his generation. He'd stop by the church, the one that was witness to his last visit before he collapsed on the sidewalk of a street in the neighborhood, on his way home.

5

I like history. My favorite subject in school was sacred history. The Bible is a wonderful book of stories and I loved to listen to the passages about Abraham and the near sacrifice of his son Isaac, ordered by a demanding and cruel God. Also, the stories of Isaac's sons Esau and Jacob, rivals for their father's love. Then there were the stories of Joseph and his brothers, not to mention the incredible destruction of Sodom and Gomorrah. Maybe that's why I was so fascinated by history, studied it, and wrote books about it. In some of my books I express opinions about the most controversial aspects of Spain's grim history. The twentieth century reached the lowest point with a civil war and two dictatorships. The second lasted forty years. It began with Catholic grassroots movements that mobilized to save what was considered the essence of Spain, its Catholicism.

In the family album, there are photos of my father wearing the Falangist uniform. Oh, how I'd like to ask him what in the world he was doing dressed in black and wearing a blue shirt with the insignia of the yoke and arrows on the collar. History doesn't come down to facts, dates, documents, speeches, and reports. History has a fundamental emotional component that explains some things more fully than simple facts. I tell my students that to understand history one needs a high degree of poetic imagination. What did a young man like my father Mariano, who was raised among the wheat fields and olive groves near Chinchón, think about politics? I know for certain he lived at a time when patriotism and nationalistic exaltation ran high and caused harm, along with the powerful presence of the church. I'm not referring to religion in general but rather those organized religions that have become institutions with far-reaching spiritual, economic, and social influence. The threat of socialism and anarchy rose like a summer cloud predicting a storm that never came. Even so, its force and lightning strikes were enough to raise flags against the menacing tempest. Thus, Europe and our home turf, Spain, tried to protect themselves against the risks of national dissolution that was filling schools with atheists, private clubs with working class members, and streets with Arabs and Africans. In other words, the threat of equal opportunity, although the greatest threat, after the loss of the American territories, was the possible dissolution of the national geography by separatist and sectarian movements. Spain would no longer be "One, Great, and Free," but a nation divided by territories, political parties, and languages. Perhaps that's what my father was thinking or maybe I'm just trying to respond to that mute dialogue that was never spoken and only sowed silence in my young restless heart. Maybe he was seduced by the flashy uniform? Uniforms impose order where disorder reigns. And while differences lead to exclusion, uniforms equalize and include, while subject to discipline.

In that family album, there are photos of my father, his hair neatly slicked back with Brillantine, a look popularized by Rodolfo Valentino, Carlos Gardel, and Mussolini, his uniform carefully ironed, and his shoes polished to a high shine. He's smiling as he walks down La Calle de Alcalá, one of the main avenues of Madrid. At his side, her arm slipped into his, walks my mother, with a sweet smile, flared skirt, low-heeled shoes, and a hopeful expression on her face, open to what life may bring as if life had no limits or destination. Her gaze is fixated on a future without bumps in the road, the way life feels when you're attached to the arm of a young, uniformed man who says the loveliest things and loves you with the passion of a convert. What kind of activism and rallies did he participate in? Did he ride around in one of those luxury cars that young Falangists drove to intimidate the rebels of the UGT and the PSOE, who, with raised fists, closed factories and stopped machinery? Did the growing violence give him pause or did it embolden him? Did he raise his hand and salute the new sun or the candle that ignited the youthful members of the Spanish Falange?

He'd just come from his hometown. He would've traveled by train on La Veloz, at twenty kilometers an hour or so, and arrived in a station on the outskirts of the city. He made his way to Gran Vía, where a woman friend of the family lived in an attic apartment that had a rooftop view of the big city. How exciting it must've been for a country boy to find himself on that street amid all that hubbub. Did he look for a job? What did he live on and how? With whom did he interact? What churches did he frequent to offset his loneliness? The war broke out when he was twenty-one years old. He was born in 1915. At one point, someone must've swayed him with political slogans about facing the sun and wearing a new shirt, mentioning a new spring, urging him to stop the chaos overrunning the streets of the city and put an end to the burning of churches and the profanation of temples. The medals, belt buckles, and felt hats of the Falangist party shine much more than the corduroy jackets and flat canvas shoes of the Republicans. What did he read? What were his favorite passages? I remember him reciting the Spanish poets

José María Gabriel y Galán and Juan Chamizo.

> I was raised in a home
> abounding in perfect bliss.
> And to have one of my own,
> I tried to be like my father.
> And searched for a woman like my mother
> among the daughters of my noble land,
> and I was like my father, and my wife was
> the spitting image of my dearly departed mother.

> (J.M. Gabriel y Galán, *Castellanas*)

I also memorized this poem, and during the years of my religious fervor, I'd recite it to my friends as we left the academy after training, or on weekends beside our campfires in the Guadarrama mountain range, between Madrid and Segovia.

But my father went away one afternoon in December of 1958. I inherited orphanhood, and never got answers to all the questions that nag me now. If only he had explained to me, if only we'd spent time together making sense of what made no sense back then, perhaps I could've told this story with something more than facts and documented this fictionalized tale.

> I was expelled from childhood
> by the strikes of a ruler,
> the clash of shattered plates,
> and a father's heart
> ruptured in the aorta.

My canine tongue
still licks the scars.
Orphanhood wafts through my study,
rounding the sweet virgin
of God knows what god,
and the books by Althusser,
next to a pipe I never smoked.

Every now and then I empty
the ashes of that distant emotion.

(From *Pureza demolida/
Ravaged Purity*)

6

Writing is something no one ever made me do. I write to understand myself, to impose order on the incoherent and tangled thoughts that wander through my mind. I believe the moment has come for me to tell this vague and elusive story that challenges my memory. I hope that among the memories distorted by time, some will do justice to this version of the story. I know that a novel is fiction, but it's based on collective memory, things that happened to someone, to a certain person, or several individuals. Together they form a compendium of history, myth, and fiction. What would we do without fiction? Without myths? We wouldn't have gods or legends, nor would we dare cross riverbeds, climb unreachable peaks, or traverse oceans.

I hope this rhetorical exercise will help me remember the boy I once was and recall that impassioned teen who adored the Christian God with fervor, only to abandon Him for the bosom of a woman. I wish to resuscitate the adult man who committed one error after another, If he's still alive with his bones intact it's only because of good fortune bestowed upon him by those guardian angels who've been my constant companions for so many decades and more years to come, or at least that's what I hope.

I've always had the feeling that we go through life blindly. We know there are streets with traffic and lights, cars that stop and go, and pedestrians whose decisive steps are taking them somewhere. Everything seems to follow a logical microcos-

mic or universal order. I think someone must've organized all
this chaos. But it hasn't been that way for me personally. A
feeling of wandering without a destination has been with me
all my life. Only in the last decade, maybe I'm exaggerating,
my deeds and actions have had a purpose or certain order.
It's curious that I feel this way when I have fewer years left
to live. I've reached the age when everything is meaningful
or savored in a different way, maybe because the end is in
sight or because the passage of time puts everything into perspective. But this is no exaggeration: time passes in childhood
and youth like the burst of an imaginary bubble. That makes
sense and is how it should be. Can you imagine a childhood
without imagination? The concepts of good and evil are un-
clear in the early years, although certain educators insist that
before children reach their first birthday, they already possess
a moral compass and know right from wrong. I'm not sure.
In my case, I noticed the selfishness of children obsessed with
the fulfillment of basic needs. And it didn't take long for me
to appreciate the depth of suffering of those around me. That's
why I shied away. The day my father died, they took me to the
house of a divorced aunt to spare me the most traumatic and
tragic moments of the funeral and burial. I don't know if they
did me a favor or helped me avoid the pain that in the long
run is a lesson to be learned.

Spanish culture has always had close ties with death.
Our Christian God is displayed in churches and temples
as a crucified god, tortured and killed. The idea is to set a
moral example. The constant reminder of death is enlightening, or so they say. His mother, Mary, appears in tears at
the foot of the cross or with her dying son lying across her
lap. And so, Christians, especially Catholics, are taught that
death is a constant presence. I spent that fateful day of my

father's death searching for ways to avoid the pain looming over my life and flee that devastating and inevitable reality. I distracted myself with thoughts that cheered me up, plans for the future, anything to relieve me of that anguish. I don't know if I cried, I don't know if I ever cried over his death. I remember that the month before, in November of 1958, the North American actor Tyrone Power had passed away. He was young and handsome like my father and had acted in the film version of Hemingway's novel *The Sun Also Rises*, about a group of young American and British ex-pats who travel from Paris to Pamplona for the Festival of San Fermín, the parties, the bullfights, and the running of the bulls. Tyrone Power was rich and famous, unlike my father. If an actor like him, who'd been married to beautiful actresses, had died at the height of his career, that only meant all of us were destined to die, including my father. He'd been married to a young and beautiful woman, my mother, who'd just turned forty when he left her a widow. She had a modest middle-class upbringing and relied on my father for many things, both material and emotional. Nevertheless, that fateful day would transform her, and she'd pick up the reins of the house to keep the ship afloat. She took on a role that she'd never assumed before. She didn't put on the pants because she never wore them. In her mind that would've been a lack of modesty. Modesty, that's the word that guided her behavior and actions. She thought a proper woman should be prudent and modest. I wonder if those were values of the time instilled with Christian precepts of Franco's Spain by the Female Section, which was charged with disseminating such principles under the watchful eye of the illustrious Pilar Primo de Rivera, whose family dominated Spanish politics and caused us so much harm. My mother, who dressed in mourning for two long years, took charge of the house and managed the family household with few resources. To do so, she had to take my sister and brother out of school at ages sixteen and fourteen, and put them to work. My grandfather Antonio and my grandmother Rosario also came to live with us and were like another set of parents in the extended family. My grandfather's nickname was El Jaro because he had light blue eyes and blond hair. He was born in Villanueva de los Infantes and was an unpretentious, hard-working man of his word. His actions were governed by a strict code of honor. He obeyed the orders of my grandmother, that spirited and energetic Andalusian in command of both their destinies. I imagine them during the Civil War, when they had to abandon their house because sirens sounded the alarm of in-coming bombing. They hurried into the tunnels of the subway, the closest refuge they could find, and, when they came out, all that remained were ruins. What did they do? Who could help them? My grandfather was a socialist, and his son, my Uncle Pepe, earned the rank of Captain of the Republican Army. During the years they lived with us, they never spoke of those things. My grandfather would only loosen his tongue on Sundays when he and his life-long friends made the rounds of the bars of the Barrio Argüelles. Only then would he let loose and repeat stories about climbing mountains, or tales of his feats of strength and prowess, or how his friends held contests to see who could eat the most *torrijas*, or that anecdote about the guy who ate a live mouse to show his bravado. Maybe my grandfather invented all that after two glasses or more of Valdepeñas wine. Both of my grandparents supported my mother and lent certain stability to the house when it seemed everything was crumbling after my father's death.

7

My grandmother left her mark on my life. She was a strong-willed woman who was never intimidated by troubles or torments. She was born in Sevilla and adopted by an aunt who raised her. She never mentioned her parents. The details are lost among photos that don't exist. Most were never taken, and the rest remained among the ruins of the house in the Moncloa neighborhood where they lived when Franco's air force bombed Madrid in one of the first punishing raids on the capital. Their house was blown to bits by that air strike. My grandmother was always sixty-something or seventy years old, or at least that's what I thought. She wore her jet-black hair streaked with gray in a bun. She dressed in black or dark colors and looked like a character from a García Lorca play, or one of those dark sullen women who comes to Spain from the Middle East. Her light shone from within. I never asked her about her origins. All of us Spaniards have African blood. That's just the way it is. One thousand two hundred years of our history confirm this. Recently, I sent a sample to a company that identifies origins through DNA. The results were what I imagined they'd be: 71% from ancestors from the Iberian Peninsula, including Portugal and southern France (the Operés seem to have descended from the south of France, when French immigrants inhabited the valleys of the Pyrenees); 16% from Italy and Greece; 4% from Ireland and Scotland; 3% from Sweden; 3% from Great Britain; 2% from North Africa, and 1% European

Jews This means I might be a descendant of an Arabic Jew with some Viking blood mixed in. Isn't that the biological make-up of most humans? The ability to trace our origins through DNA shows that purity of blood doesn't exist, not even remotely. What would Hitler have thought if he'd been informed of his possible Jewish ancestry? What purity? And what ancient blood? How would the slaveholders in different parts of the Americas have felt if they knew that African blood ran through their veins? Thanks to DNA testing, we're surprised to learn that those Neanderthal men who had ferocious features and narrow foreheads, and hunted mammoths and other prehistoric animals, live on in modern, post-industrial humans who spend our time on the internet. I like to think that my grandmother, with her dark olive skin, blackberry hair, and piercing eyes, had something of the gypsy in her, or Moorish blood, or roots in the land of the Moors. There was something exotic and enigmatic about her, like the Alhambra or the Santa Cruz neighborhood, which I've always been drawn to.

My grandmother never shrank from difficulties, setbacks, authority, or pain. She confronted calamities with an enviable courageous energy. She never had a car, nor did my parents, or any of my relatives. She crossed the urban landscape of Madrid walking at a pace that, at my young age, was hard to match. In the summers, from the Peña Grande neighborhood on the outskirts of Madrid, where she rented a very modest house, we'd walk several kilometers to the Manzanares River. There she'd take off her dress and wade into the water in her slip. She never had a bathing suit, nor did my mother, at least not since the death of my father. For my mother, life after that tragic event was reduced to remembering my dead father, raising children who'd reached that difficult age, and keeping them in the fold. She had one obsession, which came down to one message she'd repeat over and over: "there's only one way to get out of this hole we're in: study." In one way or another, she got what she wanted. The three males followed her maternal advice and received university degrees. My sister, who had an above average intelligence, worked as a secretary at an early age and then became engaged.

My relationship with my grandmother, which was always intense and irrational, continued after her death. I felt as if we understood each other in one way or another. She'd take me with her every summer to her house in Peña Grande, probably because my other aunts and uncles preferred not to take care of me. As a boy, I'd earned the reputation of a crazy rebellious kid who took dangerous risks. I liked to climb to the highest branches in the trees in our yard and smoke anise cigarettes or hoist myself up to the windows on the second floor by grabbing the bars. I'd disappear for hours when I should've been home and get into fist fights with kids in the neighborhood or at school. So, when summer arrived, the only one willing to handle me was my grandmother, that spry hardworking woman whom I know so little about. As a teenager, she'd left her aunt's house in the Triana neighborhood of Sevilla and settled in Madrid. What did she do then? With whom did she live? How did she spend her time? What did she like to do? Maybe she could dance sevillanas or a little flamenco. We can only wonder. Children don't ask questions. Some adults don't either. They talk and talk about their lives and want someone to ask them questions even though they themselves never do. My grandmother didn't go to church either. She didn't seem to have strong convictions or beliefs, except for a portrait of San Antonio that hung in her dining room. She'd maintain a running conversation with him, a one-way very informal monologue: "Good morning, how are you today, Antonio? Last night I didn't sleep well, I must go to the market and don't know if it's going to rain before I return. Should I take an umbrella?" She'd tell him about her aches and pains – her bunions – and other afflictions, but mainly she'd pray to him. She'd ask him to help someone get well, to let her lottery ticket be a winner, or help her find something she'd lost: a coin purse, her keys, scissors. If San Antonio didn't respond to her demands quickly, she'd have a fit and become angry. When she reached that point, my grandmother would flip the saint's portrait over and make him stare at the wall until she'd calm down or find what she'd lost. "All right let's make peace," she'd say, and the saint, with the halo over his head, would be returned to his original position. I don't know for certain if this anecdote is a fictionalized part of my memories or if it truly happened that way. It's possible that I've told it so many times that the story has become engraved in my memory and belongs to the chapter of real things. It's not unusual to take an anecdote that we've heard at one time and transform it into our own personal recollection. One time, I was chatting with one of my closest friends at the university, and much to my surprise, he told me a story that I'd told him previously about something that happened to me and my mother. It was a personal anecdote that was a great lesson for me. I'm not sure if my friend thought it had great didactic value and so he made it his own, something that happens to us when we teach, or if he simply thought that it had happened to him some time ago. Another time, my grandmother walked into the Church of San Antonio, perhaps to pray to her saint who was the only one she revered. A priest approached her and said, "Señora, you can't come in here without stockings." My grandmother looked at the priest's bare feet and retorted, "and you, what are you doing here without socks?"

In her old age, she'd shrink down into her old easy chair, reserved just for her. She was born in the nineteenth century, in 1890, I believe. In her very old age, she was attacked and imprisoned by Alzheimer's, that terrible disease that kills you even though you're technically still alive. My mother suffered from it too. The disease takes over the most precious part of your being, memory. Without memory we're empty vessels teeming with nothing. The eyes stare into the distance at nothing. The emotions lack any reference. Everything that has formed who we are and forged our personal history is forgotten. What remains is a deep dark menacing hole. For a while, my grandmother held conversations with the news anchors on TV. She'd greet them when they appeared on the screen, smile at them, thank them, tell them about her life, and then say goodbye when they wished everyone a good evening at the end of the program. That's how she spent the final years of her life in my childhood home because my mother refused to put her in a nursing facility where she would've received better care.

She continues to visit me after her death, or am I the one who summons her. I never visited the cemetery where she was laid to rest. Cemeteries have always seemed to me to be gloomy places that hold coffins with rotting corpses that eventually turn to dust. Above ground, tombstones, crosses, and marble stones record a name, a date, what's been forgotten. My grandmother has found a way to be present in the afterlife, normally at moments of personal or professional crisis when I need her most. She doesn't really appear, but she communicates with me through some kind of spiritual state, and without asking her for anything, she gives me a sense of peace and a feeling the problem will have a happy solution. That's how it is almost always, if not every time. Since the death of my sister, many years later, in 2005, I've felt her conciliatory presence as well. I like to think this is true. I'd like it to be so. Do they come to me or is it my desire that invokes them? They don't speak. Silence is our form of communication. My grandmother's face, that dark countenance with black eyes and her calm presence does more without speaking and manages to settle my implausible human crises. Nearly all are minor, personal problems. Perhaps everything comes down to eating (hunger is a true evil), growing, loving, crying, becoming ill, and dying. It's best to die on a sunny day descending a mountain.

As I grow older, I find myself asking more questions with no definitive answers. I search for answers not only in books but in stories we hand down from one generation to the next. For years, my brother Mariano collected our grandmother's sayings and songs, popular songs, and proverbs from the heart of Andalucía. Is this what happens to us? Are we aware of who our parents were and what they did for us? While they provide for us, they seem larger than life. They accompany and teach us and yet we don't have a clear idea of their needs, work, or passions. One day we look back without anger and gaze on a misty scene in which we catch a glimpse of fragmented acts in which our parents are the protagonists. They appear on stage, as if rehearsing a role they'd been assigned and wearing the appropriate costume for the character they were cast to portray. The father dressed as a father and the mother in her maternal frock.

The kitchen is dark,
the fire has gone out.

Deep and hollow silence of the pot,
not forgotten by the coals.
Homey scene
of scarred shelves
healed by dust.
Oh, vintage kitchen of nooks and crannies.

I enter with slow steps
from the lengthy corridor.
I stand in the venerable kitchen.
There is an age-old curtain
through which the purest memories sift,
separated by a long trench.

I root,
unearthing a trail of scents.
I look for
grains and salts, I search.
I delve
into parched legumes, probing.

I've come to this room
of fecund fragrances.
I revere with respect
the matrix and time gone by.
This is the kitchen of my youth.
Here I learned about giving,
sacred service.

(From *Acróbata de ternuras/
Acrobat of Affection*)

8

My father dressed nicely, as was the custom in his time. In photos, the few kept in the family album, he appears on a Sunday afternoon on the campus of the Universidad Complutense de Madrid, wearing a dark suit, white shirt, and tie. He's holding a little girl in his arms, my sister Lourdes. Next to him is the demure figure of my mother, wearing a suit with a jacket, also dark, a white blouse, and shoes with wide heels. It's a typical Sunday afternoon. They've gone out for a stroll, and most likely chat about their newly born daughter, the precarious labor situation, and their financial straits. They gaze at the indigo blue sky of Castille, dotted with clouds here and there. The year is 1942. The Spanish Civil War ended in April 1939 and World War II is in full swing. Still visible on the building facades of *la ciudad universitaria*, whose Moncloa campus was inaugurated in 1933 a few years before the war began, are holes left from bombings. Nearby, where that photo was taken, there stood and still stands a shrine or chapel that displays the image of a virgin. Her body is riddled with the gunshots she was subjected to during the war at the hands of Republican soldiers who defended Madrid from the advancing line of Franco's troops, erroneously called nationalists. This inappropriate appropriation of the term caused much harm to Spanish nationalism, as did the atrocities committed by Republicans, such as shooting repeatedly at the image of the Virgin Mary. My father never abandoned his Catholic faith. The day he died on a sidewalk in his neighborhood, he was returning from the church of Cristo de la Victoria.

One of the most powerful scenes that remains engraved in my memory is how he cut bread for lunch. He'd take a large round loaf of bread, and before cutting it into slices to dole out to his children, he'd make the sign of the cross over the crust and kiss it. Without a doubt, a liturgical gesture.

At the center of the table
lies the bread, a bursting heart of flour.
At either side,
hands await impatiently
and lips anticipate.

The dining room is aglow
in candlelight, sacramental table
to which we flocked,
punctual as a tolling bell,
on clear middays,
for every lunch,
on cold moonlit mornings,
and at the weary hour
that ushers in sleep.

Enter the mother. She serves.
The mighty spoon
plunges into the pot,
revered stew of holy herbs,
humble potatoes from the garden,
merciful carrots,
bloody tomatoes,
leaves of laurel freed from wreaths,

perfect infusion for the tongue.

Enter the father. He officiates.
Grand wooden table.
Old pine altar.

(From *Acróbata de ternuras/
Acrobat of Tenderness*)

The Spanish Civil War had, like all wars, an important economic component. Socialism, the anarchist trade unions,
and the proletarian revolution represented a threat to the
ruling classes that possessed power: landowners, aristocracy,
and the newly emerging industrial bourgeoisie. Nevertheless,
it was an ideological war in which religion played a principal
role. The manifestations of hatred toward the Church and
its institutions provoked acts of violence and consequential
repercussions. It's true the Church watched over souls and
purses. Owner of land and real estate, despite certain secular
laws, the Church with its strong ties to the monarchy and
the aristocracy also controlled education and morality. Spain
was a monolithically Catholic country that was reluctant to
abandon obsolete traditions as it made efforts to modern-
ize. Any attempt to do so by trade unions or intellectuals
clashed with the rigidity of the Church, which explains the
acts of vandalism against its properties, burning of temples,
and desecration of images and tombs. The military coup of
1936 purported to be a national crusade of liberation against
communism, socialism, and atheism. For conservatives,
Spain was in essence Catholic. A curious characterization,
as if a country had an original essence, as if at any given
moment in history someone could detect its primordial and

fundamental substance. Nations, like individuals, are nothing more than works in progress built on the framework of what came before. There's nothing essential or permanent about us. We're made of physical traits, tendencies, and inclinations that transform daily. Imagine a country, with all its people, institutions, and history, in a perpetual state of change. The crisis at the end of the nineteenth century, with the loss of the last colonies in America and the Philippines, represented the beginning of a new shift to delineate the course toward which Spain, the nation of all nations, was headed. The banquet was served, and the portions dished out to the many disgruntled diners. No one would emerge victorious, although multiple forms of governance were put to the test: two dictatorships, one relatively brief, and the other an exceedingly long, cruel, and painful regime that left deep scars on the parched skin of the nation. Today, in the year 2020, in which I write, the scars are still visible. New voices of new generations rise and argue that Francoism is alive and well. Those who think this way, didn't live through the Franco regime and the havoc it wreaked. Some after-effects still linger, malignant customs, authoritarian forms of behavior and corruption, bribery, and other scourges. And yet, Francoism was buried in El Valle de los Caídos, along with the corrupt body of its creator. Authoritarianism became entrenched in certain political practices. Mentalities don't change from one day to the next. The movements for secession in the Basque Country or in Catalonia, violent or not, can only be understood by examining the prohibitions and restrictions imposed on cultural expressions during the dictatorship, whether in the use of regional languages or in the limitations on forms of governance.

9

As children we invent worlds that become part of our imagination. As teenagers, our desires begin to change, but still have little to do with the reality of each passing day. They form dreams that should be preserved not cast aside. What would we do without dreams? We'd grow up too attached to sunny days, dank classrooms and the strict discipline of education, allegiance to family values, and submission to a job. I barely remember my most persistent dreams. In my first years as an errand boy for the Hilaturas de Fabra y Coats Company, I fantasized about becoming a rock star. To that end, I began the long, futile, and unattainable task of saving enough to buy an electric guitar, which I considered the first step in my rise to fame. Rock and roll, with its electric guitars, had entered the musical world with a fury, creating the greatest musical revolution of the twentieth century. Musicians like Chuck Berry, Fats Domino, and Little Richard never achieved the notoriety of Elvis Presley, so slick and cool and with that velvety voice of his and those gyrating hips that caused girls over half the planet to swoon. The Beatles and The Rolling Stones came next. When I was fifteen, my best friend Adrián had a record player, or what was called a "pick up," and we'd listen to records by Paul Anka, Jerry Lee Lewis, and other stars of the time. That's how we started the Sunday afternoon *guateques* or house dance parties. Adrián, who was savvier and more determined, would bring the record player, not his but one borrowed from the company he worked for. Few families had a record player back then. He'd also bring records and invite the girls. We'd spend the entire afternoon dancing, and for refreshments, drink Coca-Cola and other soft drinks. Neither of us knew how to dance, but we imitated the moves we saw in the movies. I have a vivid recollection of "King Creole" in which Elvis Presley showed the best of his repertoire, ripe for imitation. When the party ended, we'd go to a neighborhood bar and order glasses of ice-cold milk. We didn't consume any kind of alcohol. I didn't try that until much later. We believed milk would make us strong, a fundamental condition for playing soccer, which was the king of sports for all of us. We played soccer round the clock. We'd get to school an hour before classes started so that we could play in the schoolyard, which also had two regulation goals. We'd continue playing between classes at recess, forty boys with one ball that we'd pursue without order or direction. After school, we'd head for the garden or yard behind my house and continue playing soccer, although sometimes we chose more daring and violent games. We even signed up for try-outs for the youth soccer teams of Real Madrid, the best national team with the most championship titles and the greatest reputation in Spain, and possibly the world. Obviously, they never called us up, but we kept practicing dribbles and fancy footwork, imitating the heroes of the time, without a doubt Di Stéfano la Saeta Rubia, Gento, and Kubala, among others. On Sundays, we'd go to the Metropolitano Stadium near our house to watch the games of Atlético de Madrid. My father was a fervent loyal fan of that team, and while he was alive, we had youth membership I.D. cards. After his death, we lost that privilege and had no choice but to try to sneak in without a pass. We were able to slip in often, but sometimes the man attending the gate would take pity on our devotion and let us come in and huddle in a grassy area near the corner of one of the goals. From there, we'd observe the moves of our soccer heroes: Peiró, Escudero, Collar, and others. The old Metropolitano was a neighborhood stadium. Nothing like the modern stadiums built for today's soccer players, superstars whose fame surpasses that of Hollywood actors or popular musicians. On summer mornings, when some of our friends in the neighborhood had left to go on vacation, or spend the summer *veraneando*, as they used to call it back then, we'd watch the training practices when they let us in. It was a daily party. At the end of their practice, we'd ask for autographs. What ever happened to those autographs? And those heroes? Like most things we collect, they remain covered in dust in the corner of our memories. We struggle to retrieve them, but once we do, what good are they? We have collections of trading cards, medals, badges, photos of celebrities, calling cards, story books, coins, mementos from girl-friends, certificates, and awards. Later, after finding them, we get the feeling they've aged in those boxes in the storage room, or in our forgetful hearts. I also wanted to be an actor. The funny thing is, that on some level, I've continued my musical ambitions, getting out a guitar at family gatherings or the weddings of friends. I've also kept up with soccer as a coach for the high school team of my city Charlottesville. As for theater, that's an activity I direct at least once a year at the university. What matters most is to stay in the game.

10

I'm traveling across New Mexico from Albuquerque in a rented Hyundai Sonata with Carrie, my wife of forty years. We've spent two days in this southern state that only partially conforms to the social and cultural norms of the United States. The Hispanic and Indigenous presence (a vibrant cultural heritage of twenty Pueblo tribes) and the deep blending of both, have left a special imprint on the traditions of this ochre land. New Mexico is essentially Nuevo México. In the Indian Pueblo Cultural Center, one can read about legends and myths still preserved by the descendants of the first inhabitants of this land, which is somber and burnished, like the faces of those who built their adobe houses and erected religious center on the plateaus. In New Mexico, the Spanish presence can be felt everywhere. They even pay tribute to Spanish heroes. A massive sculpture near the museum commemorates the arrival of Juan de Oñate in 1598. He's accompanied by a troop of soldiers from the valley of Mexico, some Hispanic and others Indigenous, possibly Tlaxcaltecas (allies since the violent invasion of Hernán Cortés), along with wagons, oxen, dogs, and pigs. The names of the Indian Pueblos reflect the Spanish influence: Jemez, Sandia, Laguna, San Felipe, Santa Ana, San Ildefonso, among others. The landscape even resembles the Castilian plains.

Carrie is an anthropologist with the greatest intellectual curiosity of anyone I know. Everything interests her. I learn something new every day with her, although at times her boundless erudition irritates me. It must be my competitive spirit. Together we cross the Chihuahua Desert, one of the largest on the planet. It extends from El Paso to Mexico City. For centuries, caravans of travelers, adventurers, explorers, and Indigenous guides and porters crossed that inhospitable desert and made their way to the city of Santa Fe, the seat of the government of that extensive territory. They needed a lot of faith and luck to traverse that treacherous land where temperatures soar above one hundred degrees in the summer. The intrepid Álvar Núñez Cabeza de Vaca was the first European traveler to wander those parts. The route was given the name Camino Real. In Spain and its colonies everything was royal until the monarchy changed from absolute to constitutional. Hundreds of years passed under the yoke of an absent monarchy and a sterile aristocracy. Only a few exceptional characters were able to escape the historical trajectory marked by disdain, privileges of bloodlines, hatred, and obstacles, which together prevented any progressive initiatives. Some of the Viceroys sent to America had the ability to govern that expansive and unfamiliar territory. It's amazing that such a vast continent, from Santa Fe to Tierra del Fuego, was controlled by the Spanish Crown for more than three hundred long years with relatively little strife.

In 1848, all the territory to the north of New Spain, which had gained its independence in 1821 and called itself the United Mexican States, became part of the United States. Today the city of El Paso, on the shores of the Río Grande, is a dynamic city with one of the lowest levels of violence in North America. It's an orderly city with an uninhabited downtown like so many other downtowns in cities across this country. A city with tall skyscrapers that house the headquarters of banks and other financial institutions, and whose crystal panes look down on parks or plazas where the homeless snooze.

On the other side of the Río Grande, behind several metal border walls, lies Ciudad Juárez. The population is nearly equal, but Ciudad Juárez is one of the cities with the highest crime rate in the country, infamous for the disappearance of young women who were murdered like trophies of war by members of the cartel. Much has been published about these disappearances in the press, and in Roberto Bolaño's masterpiece, *2666: A Novel.* How do you explain this? Where does evil end and good begin? What is the dividing line? Poverty? Injustice? Who has a stronghold on justice? Under what myths is civic morality constructed, or in its absence, where does the dividing line between these two ways of life, become blurred?

In my parents' humble house, I learned basic principles about solidarity, honesty, and collective justice, which aren't necessarily related to political ideologies. It's easier to share poverty than wealth. My father was a conservative Catholic Falangist, and my mother was born into a Socialist Republican home. How did those two opposites unite to raise good children, in the true sense of the word good, as Antonio Machado used to say?

I write to get to the bottom of this long history of parents, ancestors, children, Spain and America, the divide separated by the Atlantic, and immigrants crossing dangerous borders that in the past were merely imaginary lines. I walk this land to understand what the dust left behind. My readings of chronicles are an invitation for reflection and adventure. Slowly but surely the adventures of my life have become more limited in range. I need to focus on every stone and pebble and cast aside the images that cloud my gaze. The desert seems to encompass basic elements, but an infinite wondrous world of flora and fauna waits to be discovered with the eyes and the nose. We see so little, only that which we understand or what interests us. The rest is just a blurry film.

11

I realize I've spent more than half my life in the United States. I wonder how this country has impacted the man I have become. For some, I still sound like a Spaniard when I speak English with a heavy accent I've never lost. For others, the gringo influence is obvious. What I honestly believe is I'm a citizen of the world who's witnessed its rampant globalization. I'm an inhabitant of this world of more than seven and a half billion human beings who are in contact with each other like never before and live in a precarious situation. In my case, I have attempted, with success, to avoid being a tourist who visits cities and takes photographs. I've tried to be a resident, not a tourist, an adopted son with a multicultural heart that beats to different rhythms and synchronized emotions.

As I write this, the United States is immersed in the largest wave of deportations in its history. Worse than his predecessors, Trump's administration has created detention centers for children separated from their deported parents. No one can determine the consequences of these immigration policies, which are an inhumane punishment that will leave deep scars on those children and on this country that I admired when I came here in 1978. Somehow, the admiration I once felt has slipped through my fingers and the respect has been tarnished. What happened? This is where modern democracy was invented, where the declaration of human rights was written, and where the constitution with the greatest influence in the world was drafted, the inspiration for so many other constitutions in the Americas and elsewhere. Carrie laments the profound sadness and shock brought on by recent political events and insists that we are witnessing a new fall of the Roman Empire. As with all empires in decline, reactions to politics become intense and explosive, reverting to hatred, xenophobia, and repression. Borders are closed, communication is suppressed, aspects of identity are recast, molded to fit the image of the group in power or the minority with influence. I'd like to think it's a dangerous tide that will give way to something better, or perhaps not. Maybe the country has always held that arrogant and domineering bias that determines the actions of the current president. I recall the presidencies of Jimmy Carter and Barak Obama, and I see an olive branch at my window. I think about my children and grandchildren and the legacy they will receive. For now, they are fine.

My mother liked the tranquility of autumn in Virginia. She'd pick up colorful leaves from the ground to show her sister Pura in Zamora and her children in Madrid, when she recounted tales of her trip. Her own story always revolved around the family, her children, grandchildren, and daughters-in-law. Everyone one else were outsiders to be treated with the strict code of decency and good manners. The Civil War raged when she was seventeen years old, the years of her youthful beauty, rebellion, flirtation with boyfriends, parties, dances, and maybe one folly or another. When she passed away, the country was still in the hands of Bill Clinton, during his second administration. He was a president with sex appeal and charisma, and a democrat who meant well but couldn't escape the scandals of his extramarital indiscretions. Things started to heat up in the country and the rich got richer. My mother always fought against inequalities and injustice in her own way. During the Civil War, she managed to confront shortages of everything and survived without losing her joy for life. She once hit a woman on the head with her umbrella when the greedy customer tried to take the last kilo of sardines at a fish store where my mother had been waiting her turn for nearly an hour. That was one of her few rebellions. She left us before she could see the senseless mire in which the world has become entangled.

12

I became a father at twenty-four in the most unexpected and irresponsible way. What I'm trying to say is I fathered a child by pure chance, although paternity was always a romantic fantasy of mine since early adolescence. Perhaps I was influenced by poetry, by the poems of Gabriel y Galán and Luis Chamizo that my father used to recite, and years later, by my readings of Miguel Hernández, especially his poems from *Vientos del pueblo* (*Wind of the People*): "Onion Lullabies" and "Song of a Soldier Husband," among many others.

I have sown your womb with love and seedlings,
perpetuating the echo of blood to which I respond
while waiting over the furrow like the plow awaits:
I have reached the roots.

(From "Canción del esposo soldado"/
"Song of a Soldier Husband")

The poetry of Hernández evokes all the elements of that physical love rooted in the earth and transformed into the body of the woman. His poetry is erotic and religious at the same time, despite his Republican affiliation and popular appeal. Through love, Hernández goes to the source and looks toward the future, exalted by a kiss, a mouth, and teeth.

Mouth that sweeps my mouth along,
mouth that carries me away,
mouth that comes from afar
to shine your light on me. [. . .]

Kiss that roams in the shadow:
kiss that wanders
from the first cemetery
to the last stars.

(From *Cancionero y romancero de ausencias/
Songbook and Ballads of Absences*)

I discovered Hernández by accident during the period I suffered through the obligatory training in the Spanish Army. Franco's army was a rusty bureaucratic machine comprised of hundreds of generals and officers who provided no service but received benefits for their absolute allegiance to the regime. To keep that gang of generals satisfied and under control they received good salaries with bonuses. Their mission amounted to keeping peace in the Sahara, guarding the Moroccan border, and little else. The Spanish military was not part of NATO, and, for this reason, the Spain's barracks were full of soldiers without a mission. Their activities were primarily for show: standing guard, marching in parades of national pride, pledging allegiance to the flag, and protecting the bases from potential enemies. The more soldiers there were, the easier it was to justify the excess of officers, generals, colonels, commanders, captains, lieutenants, ensigns, sergeants, and the list goes on and on. Since the end of the Civil War in 1939, military service was obligatory for all twenty-one-year-old males. At that age, the lives of young men were interrupted, no matter their activities or commitments. They were sent to recruitment and training centers where the mantra was blind obedience to authority. Training boiled down to two things: discipline and obedience. I volunteered for the draft so that I could choose where I'd be stationed. I needed to stay in Madrid, near my house so that I could continue working at the company and make money to support the family.

My memories of that time in the army are tragicomic. They amount to submission to officers of mediocre intelligence and preparation who forced us to repeat senseless drills. Not a single officer stood out as a model worthy of emulation. Just the opposite. For months, I tutored a sergeant who was trying to earn his high school degree, giving him private lessons on everything from grammar to history, and mathematics. It was an impossible undertaking. In fact, he arrested me if I didn't provide the possible questions he'd have to answer on the next exam.

Perhaps the silver lining in those ill-fated years was my encounter with Miguel Hernández. It happened one afternoon at base camp in the town of Mósteles, while we lined up for one of the many useless exercises that we were subjected to at all hours of the day. A soldier my age, whom I barely knew, took out a book from the pocket of his raincoat and asked me, do you know this poet? I could see his name out of the corner of my eye and opened the book and after reading only one of the poems, I felt awestruck. I asked if I could borrow the book, and devoured it, reading the poems over and over again. I memorized some of them and while we marched to the fruitless shooting sessions with Mauser rifles, I'd repeat them in my head. The paternal feeling is very powerful and bold for Miguel Hernández. And so, my romantic fantasies weren't obsessed with the body of a woman, but rather focused on the woman and the son. This explains, in part, my lunacy, which turned out to be a watered-down form of romanticism.

Shortly after discovering Hernández, I started to write poems inspired by that lyrical vitality. I wrote them for my first love, the woman with whom I shared my first intimate relationship. They were poems that clearly imitated my passion for Hernández, in which blood, earth, skin, and fluids converged in a sensual symphony. I'd send her those compositions concocted during my youth. The truth is I knew nothing about sex, how to do it or how it worked. During the Franco regime, sexuality was taboo. It couldn't be portrayed, taught, or mentioned in conversations. Needless to say, no sex education was offered in school. My father, who should've been my source of information and education, had been long buried. My mother was too modest and prudent to talk about such things. That's why my first experiences with sex were a string of failed encounters. I masturbated like crazy and went to confession nearly every day because masturbation was considered a mortal sin that could send me straight to hell. Who could free me from such guilty pressure? I kept no copies of the verses I sent my beloved, which must have ended up in some trash can. I did save other poems in a folder that I entitled "El hijo es la tercera dimensión de tu costado"/ "The Son is the Third Dimension of your Side," a manuscript I keep in a trunk in the attic of my house in Virginia.

The other master from those years, is one of my favorite poets, Antonio Machado. That great poet, philosopher, and intellectual who wrote reflective ad tranquil verses taught me the symbolic importance of nature as a means of revealing feelings and emotions. He was unlucky at love. His romantic experiences were at best immature, almost infantile, I would venture to say, a kind of romanticism that only his reflective restraint makes palatable. At the age of thirty-four, he fell in love with Leonor, a girl who was only fifteen years old. In his later years, he fell for a married woman, Pilar de Valderrama, the Guiomar of his posthumous verses, with whom he maintained a solely platonic relationship, even though he made her the subject of his poetic compositions. In Machado's poetry, there is no flesh, or sex, or body, only evocative watermarks between the lines.

These were my romantic influences, kneaded with doses of Christian repression. And so, when I first discovered the body of a woman and touched breasts for the very first time, the earth moved, and I had no other interests or goals. God and my religious beliefs, which had been so strong between the age of sixteen and twenty, fell by the wayside. God disappeared and was replaced by the female body, which I approached with grand clumsiness. My educational plans were also hindered because I expended all my physical and mental energy on the object of desire, during those years when one is no longer an adolescent but not yet an adult. In my first acts of intercourse, I spilled semen without remembering its ability to procreate. I was very lucky for a while, longer than can be expected, and my beloved didn't get pregnant until after that first marriage, another of my follies carried out without forethought or a game plan.

73

13

Living with a partner is one of the most complicated juggling acts to which we *homo sapiens* subject ourselves. It's not in our genetic code. In certain societies, it's a deeply rooted custom, but a particularly abnormal one when imposed by law. Living with the same person for decades requires a constant practice of generosity, dexterity, and submission to trivial norms not everyone can accept. I found a partner at an early age, but that first cohabitation didn't exceed nine months. The marriage lasted longer than desired primarily because divorce didn't exist in Spain back then, and we had to endure a very expensive ordeal to have it annulled by the Church. No doubt, the failure was due in part to our incredible immaturity, as well as other obscure reasons. I was twenty-two and she was nineteen. When I think about it, I realize it was an act of sheer madness, like so many others in my life. It lasted until the novelty and curiosity wore off. How quickly young love slips away when it's not nurtured! Once illness, personal crisis, and deception on many levels were overcome, the reality of what the marriage was not set in. The lack of sexual intimacy, the religious crisis for both of us, and the desire for independence all converged in an unfortunate union. The dilemma we faced was to break up or get married. Although disillusionment had already set in, we got married anyway. There was no rational hand or voice of authority to make us see the folly we were about to commit. Oh, Father, once again your silence. No advice comes from the tomb and the experience of your marriage was of no use to us. Even our so-called "happy honeymoon" was bitter as bile. From that deranged, premature, and inconceivable marriage, we conceived a daughter, Marta, who is the most beautiful outcome of that ephemeral union. She's now a mature, serene, and intelligent woman who faces life with wonder and a considers things with an appropriate dose of skepticism. She loves simple things, and those simple things love her.

The second marriage has lasted more than forty years. Those four decades have seen it all: happiness, three children, six grandchildren, quarrels, mutual influence, personal growth, and copious amounts of understanding and compromise. The exercise has not yet ended. We continue walking together, although at times I veer off the path. I don't consider that perverse. That could be because men build bridges, design houses, embrace conquests, and explore new routes, or invent them. Women, on the other hand, make nests. As new brides, they begin to build those nests, and looking back, they realize their mothers weren't so unbearable after all, and come to appreciate their sacrifices and losses. Thus, strand by strand, stick by stick, they build a nest, their nest. They hang photos of the family, select colors for the curtains and bedspreads, choose lamps and easy chairs, and scent everything with their personal fragrance, an essence that reflects their own tastes. Even in these postmodern times in which men share in the chores of the house, husbands continue to be nothing more than witnesses, guests who inhabit that nest in which they sleep, have breakfast, and watch television. Occasionally they propose a trip or a vacation. Otherwise, they'd disrupt an order that must be part of a genetic code.

I've always been the cook in our house. It was something I took charge of because I liked it and felt it was one way I could share in the household chores. I began to cook during my first days of independence so as not to starve to death after leaving the maternal home. Because I have a habit of not reading instructions, I never followed a recipe. I used to call my mother and ask her for family recipes, the ones I remembered from those homecooked meals of hers that I loved so much. Little by little, I figured out the basic elements of gastronomy. There aren't that many and once you learn them, it's easy to guess how to make certain dishes and recipes and even determine the origin of the flavors. The fundamental question is, what's in it? But I never entered the realm of *new cuisine*. To do that you must give up being self-taught and begin to read recipes, and even dedicate your heart and soul to that activity. I've always leaned toward traditional cooking, those familiar dishes prepared since the beginning of time in the Iberian Peninsula.

This is related to who I am. I've always resisted being pigeon-holed as to what I do professionally and otherwise. And so, this is how I came to be a jack of all trades and a master of none. I tried to be a dramatic actor who plays soccer, a soccer coach who writes poetry, a poet who teaches history, an historian who's into theater, an actor who climbs mountains, a mountain climber who rides bikes, a cyclist who writes scholarly essays, a professor who cooks, a cook who plays the guitar, and so on. But to be honest, I should say that at least I'm consistent. I've never thrown in the towel, and I've always tried to keep learning and perfecting whatever I do, without being labeled for any one activity. That's why whenever I'm asked about my profession, I always have a hard time defining myself. An old friend of mine, who was a colleague at a school in Barcelona where we both taught, filled in the little box for profession on his ID with "salesman," clarifying that he was a salesman of ideas. That's not a bad response. I must say the profession of "professor" is perhaps the one I've put in the little box most often, and the one that expresses with most accuracy my professional and vocational inclinations. As for marital commitment, I've been living under the same roof for more than forty years and counting. Like a marathon, I'm in it for the long haul.

14

My first job in education was as a teacher of mime and body language at a school for children in Barcelona, while I was still studying at the university. What did I know about mime or body language? I'd seen Marcel Marceau, the great master of mime, at several international festivals. YouTube didn't exist back then so I couldn't watch recordings of mime artists and play them over and over to imitate their techniques. I applied for the job, declaring I had previous experience. I had to give a demonstration before a committee of evaluators comprised of administrators, students, professors, and the headmaster. I accepted the offer and practiced in front of a mirror at home. Somehow, I managed to overcome the obstacles, I don't know how, and became a fabulous "teacher of body language and mime," that was my title – while working in the mornings as a salesman for a publicity agency. Given teaching mime requires no words, I was able to hang on to that job for two years. It was a school in Barcelona, in the final years under Franco, when all classes were taught in Catalan. The dictatorship knew how to be flexible when it was convenient, as it was with the upper-class Catalonian society who had helped the nationalists win the war.

Theater can light a fire like no other media, despite the rise of YouTube, Netflix, and cinema. It's been a part of my life ever since I acted in plays in high school. Years later, inspired and seduced by independent traveling theater troupes who put on shows in the final decades of the regime, I organized a theatrical group and started to direct plays with no previous experience or preparation, relying on pure intuition. In Spain, theater was not part of the university curriculum, and never has been, and given its rebellious and subversive power, Schools of Dramatic Art were frequent targets of censorship. About that time, *Primer Acto*, an excellent journal of dramatic criticism and theory, began to publish articles on directing and staging of plays by foreign troupes, texts by vanguardist authors, interviews, analytical essays, and information about performances in other countries. I bought a subscription and devoured every one of the issues with the devotion of a convert. There's nothing more dangerous and unstable than a convert. I read about Antonin Artaud and his Theater of Cruelty, the Dadaism of Alfred Jerry, Fernando Arrabal's Theater of Panic, the theories of The Living Theater proposed by Judith Malina and Julian Beck, as well as those of Grotowski and Stanislavsky, among others. Whenever I could afford it, I'd go to the theater, especially to international festivals. In the summer, I'd camp out around Avignon, in southern France, and wander its streets and plazas, admiring any form of drama or music that I happened upon. The Avignon festival, founded in 1947, was and still is the great celebration of theater that pays homage to the genre.

The first play I dared to stage was *The Investigation* by Peter Weiss, which deals with the concentration camp at Auschwitz, a powerful script based on the trials of the Nazis who ran the extermination camps. It's an accusatory play that provokes critical thinking. Perhaps the theater seduced me for that very reason because at that time in my life I was becoming more conscious about the outside world. I also mounted some short plays by García Lorca. Everything was homespun and thrown together spontaneously with barely any funds, which called for simple and creative solutions. This is the kind of theater I love, one that creates scenes with basic elements using allusion as the primary tool. I go to the theater in New York quite often to catch a Broadway musical or an off-Broadway show. These are productions in which technology plays a key role, grand dramatic spectacles that the movie industry has yet to sideline.

I saw the performances of the most experimental troupes during the María Guerrero theater festivals held in Madrid at the end of the 1960's and beginning of the 1970's. I had no interest at all in the bourgeoise comedies in vogue in Spain, in which the popular playwright Alfonso Paso dominated the billboard, with four different comedies playing at the same time. Censorship controlled what was playing and would scuttle any attempt to veer from the parameters of the comedy of manners or Golden Age plays. Emboldened and motivated by the new theatrical groups, I pursued a fantasy and embarked on an exciting adventure that was doomed to failure. I packed my little white 4x4 Renault with a few belongings and departed from my apartment in Barcelona, on Castillejos Street, and headed for Prague. That was the home base of the Laterna Magika theatrical project, whose performances had fascinated me in Barcelona. They embraced a form of mute artistic expression based on contemporary dance and body language influenced by mime, music, the cabaret, a kind of multimedia theater with a touch of magic. My goal was to be accepted into the school that trained the group and learn their techniques. What did I know about Prague back then, which was still under the yoke of communism? What did I know about the dramaturgy of Laterna Magika?

I was driven by fascination and a determination that was absolutely impulsive. I don't know what remains of that energy. How do the passing years quell our passions and subdue our dreams? Have I become so middle-class that I prefer to stay at the best hotels and eat in the best restaurants? What remains of my hippie years? I drove my run-down Renault over the highways of Europe with a force of energy unmatched by my car or wallet. When I made it to the border, Czechoslovakia was still one undivided country. They made me shave my beard because the photograph on the passport didn't match the one on my visa. On the passport, I appeared clean-shaven, my youthful countenance open for adventure. On the visa and in person, a long black beard added years to my face and cast a shadow on my gaze. And so, right there at the border, a woman with the face of a Siberian Madonna took on the role of barber and shaved off my revolutionary beard without a second thought. Those were the years that followed the assassination of Che Guevara in a Bolivian jungle without a fair trial. The bearded, long-haired image of Che became the obligatory banner and guidepost of all young men with a desire for change. My poor mother seeing me looking like Che, sporting a beret, beard, and pipe, gave up and said nothing more than "but son."

Prague seemed to me a worn-down city with grandiose buildings corroding with decay, wide avenues and gardens, and monuments and towers reminiscent of the sumptuous city it once was. The deterioration was evident even in the downtown areas. Russian troops guarded the entrances to the city and the crossroads of the main thoroughfares. They had remained in the country since the liberation movement initiated by Alexander Dubcek in the so-called Prague Spring. That period of freedom came to an end in 1968 when troops and tanks invaded the country under the Warsaw Pact. They were threatening my theatrical adventure there and forcing me to abort it, perhaps for my own good. One never knows. When I made it to the building of the drama school, the home base for Laterna Magika, what I feared was confirmed. The drama school and the departments of humanities at the university had been shut down temporarily. That order could last months or years, as indeed it turned out to be. Finding myself in a quandary, I drank liters of beer in cheap restaurants, which was served without my asking for it, along with cabbage and potato stew. Then I started the slow trip back to Barcelona, taking solace in Vienna, Venice, and Milan.

Back in Barcelona, I saw a newspaper ad soliciting actors for a theatrical company in Hospitalet de Llobregat, a working-class neighborhood in the city. I auditioned. They had me do a reading and cast me in the role of King Ferdinand in Alberto Miralles's play, *Versos de arte menor por un varón ilustre o CataroColón*. They were a group of resolute amateurs, some with more experience than others, and together we put on plays in our local venue and at festivals in nearby towns. In one of them, I was awarded the prize of Best Actor. Things looked promising. So perhaps theater was to be my future, I told myself. My unstable economic circumstances and the precarious situation of theater in Spain those days, with its strict censorship, did not bode well for guaranteeing a daily plate of lentils. And so, I opted for academic life without ever putting aside my passion for the stage and the action behind the scenes, a motivating force for me all these years. When I came to the United States, I got the bug again and put together a small theatrical group. We performed our first plays in a café near the university, and later, on stages in Charlottesville, and on the UVA campus. Since 1981, I've staged fifty-two plays. I'm still directing plays, one or two a year, with the condition that the plays be written and performed in Spanish.

I have a tough time giving up projects, activities, or people. I've never abandoned a girlfriend, they've always dumped me. If I like something or commit to something, I stick with it with an almost absurd tenacity. A therapist I once consulted told me that to make up for my father abandoning me and leaving me desolate, I'm not willing to let anything or anyone go. I wonder how hard it'll be for me when the time comes for the last journey. I'm afraid I won't be able to tell that tale or write about it.

That adventure in Czechoslovakia marked my first grand tour of Europe: Bern, Munich, Prague, Vienna, Venice, Milan, and the Italian Alps. It was a meaningful tour, although it left me with a strange bitter taste for the communist society, perhaps egalitarian, I'm not sure, but certainly sad and objectionable. I came from a dictatorship, so please don't tell me anymore what I should do, in what bed I can sleep, and with whom I can share my passions. Venice was a different matter. Who doesn't fall in love with Venice? I slept in the car or in a makeshift tent. The adventurous travel worm got under my skin and is still there inciting new adventures around the world that have been the greatest source of inspiration. The impact can be seen in my poetry, or at least that's what the critics say. I don't know where I get it from. My father never left the Iberian Peninsula. His journeys were to Villaconejos, near Chinchón, where his brother lived, and to Talavera de la Reina in Toledo, where his sister resided, and not much beyond that. In a photo in the family album, he appears in a bathing suit, running on a beach or by some stream of the Sierra de Madrid. We used to walk to the Río Manzanares in Somontes, carrying food so we could save on bus fare for the entire family. He took the last trip in Charon's boat at an early age. As far as I know, he never took an interest in theater, nor did my mother, but they say my maternal grandfather loved the *chotis* and would attend local dances to practice the steps. To everyone's surprise, the theater bug is still alive.

15

Journeys disorient and confront us with the absurdity of our personal beliefs, seducing us with something new and strange and offering a dialogue with the other, with otherness, with that one who I am not. As we travel, we cross borders and broaden the horizons of our small world through our encounters. Wasn't that how it was for the first Homo Sapiens? At the university, I teach courses on travelers, one on travelers in the Americas and another on the great travelers of the world: the Buddhist explorer Far Hsien who crossed the Asian continent in 301 b. C; the impressive seafaring expeditions of the Chinese Admiral Zheng He, between 1405-1433, which took him to the coast of eastern Africa; the legendary journeys of Marco Polo, between 1272 and 1332, and of course, those of Christopher Columbus, Magellan, Bartolomé Díaz, Francisco de Orellana, and Alexander Von Humboldt, among many others. Without explorers, we'd still be wandering in a haze across the African savannah. Their adventures fascinate me, and with a good dose of poetic imagination, I try to emulate them.

Children of the poor don't travel. They don't go to the mountains or the sea or set up umbrellas on the beach and splash around in the waves. They don't take afternoon strolls without a destination or sit at an open-air café to enjoy grilled shrimp and a soda. A recent study in the United States revealed that 28% of North Americans have never left the state in which they live. In Spain, half the population, has never traveled to another country. I was seventeen years old when I first saw the sea. I traveled with a Catholic organization I'd joined called *Hogar del Empleado*, later known as the *Movimiento Católico de Empleados*. It was created to provide education and religious opportunities to improve the lives of young workers, those who, like me, ran errands for businesses of all types for a paltry salary. Be it as it may, I saw the sea and its foam filled my heart. It was on the Cantabrian coast, in Asturias. We arrived at a seaside town whose name I can't remember, Ribadesella perhaps, and we got off the buses and walked down a gravel road toward the shore. The sea crashed against the rocks, battering them repeatedly as if to declare, I am the sea. I remember feeling an intense emotion beating in my chest. It was a planned excursion, but I never anticipated the sea would have the power to stir my emotions. Ever since then, I've been moved by the sea, ports, and the aquatic destinies awaiting me.

It has no houses with trees
or neoclassic arches.
It lacks monuments, gardens,
fields sown with wheat
or red poppies.
It doesn't adorn itself with spring flowers
or bedazzle in autumn colors.
It seems to have been severed
from a translucid immutable sky.

It's blue, light-green, indigo at times,
and perfumed with its own scent.
It never rests and seems to rock
with a cadence that calms the gaze
and delights the eye.

Its song is deep and abiding.
It sings of water, oceanic peace, origin,
resurrection, and final journey.

Its love never falters or turns bitter.
Patient, like the perfect lover,
it heartens the afternoon and rejuvenates the morn.
This is the sea that engulfs me
while awestruck I contemplate
the everlasting nocturnal waves.

(From *La vuelta al mundo en 80 poemas*/
Around the World in 80 Poems)

Many more years would pass before my mother would get her first glimpse of the sea. She must've been in her sixties when she had the chance to go to the beaches of the Levante region, about four hundred kilometers from Madrid. Her world had revolved around the streets of the city in the Argüelles neighborhood, La Moncloa, El Parque del Oeste, and the area around the university, which at that time bore witness to the aftermath of the bombing, a harsh punishment for a city that had resisted the violent attack of the military coup. The Republic had tried to transform the hierarchies and privileges of a minority in a few brief years and follow in the footsteps of its avant-garde European neighbors who began the process of modernization decades earlier. My mother was born in Madrid from emigrant parents, a carpenter from La Mancha, and a woman from Sevilla who made her way to Madrid who knows why. The war caught up with my mother during the trying years of adolescence, dashing any desires to see the world. Bombs crumbled walls of houses, church spires, as well as obstinate notions of idealism and hopes for educational reform. She endured hunger and searched among the ruins for a little bit of hope with which to rebuild a life, with a man by her side. She worked hard and found a man, married, had a daughter, then two, three, four children in a row, with barely time in between for a breather. She cooked nonstop and bought basic staples with a ration card to make much out of nothing in the kitchen. Her knuckles turned red from washing clothes with a bar of olive oil soap. She had no time to visit the sea that surrounded the peninsula within a day's journey. Vacations were spent with walks through El Parque del Oeste, near our house, and every now and then seeing a movie at the local theater. When her husband died, the sea slipped even further away. The tired old Río Manzanares became polluted with debris and wasn't worth visiting to cool off in the summer. No doubt, its contaminated waters never reached the sea.

When I moved to Catalonia to start a new phase of my life, I looked for a job and took night classes at the University of Barcelona. That's when I had the chance to spend my days with the sea, nearly every day. All I had to do to greet the sea was walk down the Ramblas, which at that time had no tourists, and go past the statue of Columbus that presided over the port. Many weekends, my friends and I would go to the beaches of the Costa Brava, above Blanes. We'd sleep on the sand and enjoy the waves in the early morning hours. We'd take a bunch of books and read texts by Althusser, Gramsci, and Martha Haneker. Those were the years of coming and going like the waves, of Marxist readings, and believing we were fighting against the dictatorship, while also pursuing the ardent bodies of young women whose creed, like ours, was freedom of thought and love.

I invited my mother to visit me on several occasions. I suppose she stayed at the house I shared with friends. Those memories seem blurry. My mother was always ready for the next blow, and for this reason she'd duck at any unexpected noise. Even in her final years, when she'd feel the rumble of a storm, she'd run and lock herself in the bathroom. It was the agonizing memory of those days when sirens announced the oncoming bombs about to assault the capital. She loved to travel. She'd gaze with wonder at the landscape through the window of a train, bus, or my Renault 4x4, which surely seemed to her a luxury she could never afford. How proud she was of the success of her sons. We'd travel with my brother José Luis to Ampurias in Gerona and to the Greek ruins whose stones had been witnesses to many landings, ravaging waves, and salty afternoons. We also traveled by boat to Mallorca, crossing the sea at night on a journey guided by stars and mermaids. As luck would have it, while we were in a small bay surrounded by mountains, the sea suddenly became enraged. My mother, whose modesty never allowed her to wear a bathing suit or get into the water, was sitting in a chair on the beach, when a rogue wave surged over the small inlet, sweeping a bunch of tourists into the sea. Amid chaos, shouts for help could be heard and, in the distance, arms appeared flailing over waves. Without thinking, I dove into the water and with some help we managed to pull a good many bathers to shore. Just when it seemed everyone was safe, someone standing on the rocks above us, pointed to a person in the water who appeared and disappeared with the swell. I dove in again toward the drowning man. I was frightened, not sure what to do once I reached him because I'm not a great swimmer and never had any experience as a lifeguard. After a few minutes that seemed eternal, I reached the body, which luckily for me was unconscious. I grabbed him under the arms and struggled to get him to shore. He wasn't breathing and seemed as if he'd swallowed the entire Mediterranean Sea. Everyone stared without moving until Carrie, my girlfriend, tried to revive him with mouth-to-mouth resuscitation. And it worked. The silent survivor began to cough, and water poured out of his nose and mouth. My mother, who'd never seen the sea, contemplated its fury and witnessed the rescue with emotion. I suppose she visited the sea other times during summer vacations with my sister Lourdes and her grandchildren. Times had changed and her old age provided opportunities she didn't have as a child, a young girl, or a wife.

16

The calendar marked the 31st of December 1999. We decided to climb the Appalachians in the Blue Ridge Mountains, on the Eastern coast of the United States. We set off, bundled in warm clothes, to spend the night and wait for the first light of dawn that would herald the arrival of the new century. We sat there excited to glimpse the first ray of the sun while listening to The Beatles' "Here Comes the Sun." The 21st century promised to be free of harm, conflict, and the neocolonial inequality passed down after World War II. A somewhat better world. We must've learned something, I told myself. It's not possible for the horrors of the 20th century to repeat themselves. But they repeated and multiplied. It began with a tragedy that shocked the USA, with a violence never before experienced or suffered in this country. It was the morning of September 11, 2001. Out of the blue, an American Airlines plane crashed into one of the Twin Towers of the World Trade Center in Manhattan, unleashing a chain reaction of panic.

My beautiful son Philip, who'd recently turned twenty-three, lived six blocks from the towers, in Battery Park. That morning he was in his apartment waiting for the hour to leave for work. Only a year before, he'd graduated from the university and had moved with his girlfriend to the big city to pursue his youthful dream of acting in theater. Like all aspiring actors in New York, he earned a living as a waiter and signed up for one audition after another, with the hope of landing a role, no matter how minor, in a Broadway or Off-Broadway play. From his bedroom in the apartment, he heard the explosion and went up to the rooftop to see what had happened. From there, he called to tell us about the inconceivable, almost absurd events that were unfolding and, while speaking with his mother, he witnessed the second plane crashing into the other tower. At that moment, residents were told to evacuate his building. I was at the university that morning getting ready for class. Carrie called me to let me know what had happened. I got on the internet to search for more information. At that instant, I received an email from Germán Yanke, a dear friend who directed the magazine *Época* in Madrid. He asked me if I had any firsthand information to share and I told him my son Philip lived very close to the towers, that he'd just called us, but had to hang up because they were evacuating his building. With my heart still in my throat, trembling with the anguished fear of a father, I quickly wrote this text, which was published in the magazine in its next issue:

LETTER TO THAT OTHER ONE

As I write, no matter where you are, the island of Manhattan is being evacuated. Chaos seems to dominate the daily hustle and bustle of that unique city, a horrible victim of indiscriminate terror. Seven days ago, just seven days, I was there, amazed as always by that cloud of energy that envelops Manhattan. There's always something distinct about this no man's city because Manhattan is a city that welcomes everyone, a flawed example of transnational globalization. I went to visit my son Philip, who lives in Manhattan, six blocks from the World Trade Center, an aspiring actor eager to embrace life fully at the tender age of twenty-three.

This morning, a few hours ago, my frightened son called to tell his mother and me that his building had been evacuated after two planes had crashed into the World Trade Center and exploded. He told us about it on the phone after witnessing the terrible event with his own eyes. He was on the street as the infernal debris spiraled down from the towers onto the avenues below and rose into the New York sky. Then the call got cut off, and moments later the first majestic tower crumbled, followed shortly afterwards by the second. The rubble must have scattered all around for blocks. My feeble imagination doesn't allow me to grasp the dimension of the tragedy or the anguish that overcomes me in this moment. While I write these lines, I try to call him, but Philip no longer answers. I dial his number over and over in vain. I know his apartment building has been evacuated and can glimpse its silhouette in the few images shown on television, but I keep trying. I call his cellphone, hoping to hear his voice. I want to hear his voice, the beautiful voice of an actor and my son so that some meaning can return to this absurd morning.

It's 11:00. Time for my first class. I walk to the classroom carrying my notes. I open the door. Thirty young tearful faces look at me. Bewilderment in their eyes.

They want an explanation. Do they expect one from me? I try to say a few words, something like what's happening is so terrible and I suggest we talk about it, something, anything that might calm our nerves. A futile proposition. Tears of incomprehension flow. I tell them I haven't been able to get in touch with Philip, that I've called him, but the line's always busy. It's just that there is no commu-

nication. I confess and share the fears of a father with them. Only two years before, Philip had sat in these same classrooms. No one can speak. A tear preempts every word. In the 25 years I've been teaching at the university never have I experienced anything like this. It's the fear of the unknown, it's the threat of a masked other, it's the senseless despair invading our daily lives.

Our first reaction is to cast blame on someone. But the thing is Philip doesn't answer, and I'm thinking about him and feel him near me. The thing is, they're clearing out Manhattan while all the airports are shutting down, and I end up canceling my class because nothing seems to make sense in the face of this indiscriminate terror.

(*Época*, September 14-20, 2001)

Ever since that day, the world hasn't been the same. The world is never the same. Nor are we. Every year, each tick-tock of the clock leaves another wrinkle on the face, traces furrowing and eroding the skin and the heart. The United States, the great colossus of the 20th century, the empire erected over the ruins of World War II, suffered an attack on its own soil for the first time in its modern history. Up until then, no one had dared. Its president in 2001, George W. Bush, a mediocre character, timid and uninformed, felt he should do something and heeded the redemptive voices of the extreme right. He searched for a scapegoat upon which to unleash his ire and frustration and found one among the many dictators with imperial ambition who abounded in the world. He accused Iraq and its president Saddam Hussein of being involved in the attack and without delay ordered the bombing of the capital Bagdad to quench his thirst for revenge. Today we know that Iraq didn't have nuclear arms of mass destruction and that Hussein had nothing to do with the attacks. Another olive branch was broken, and another age of innocence lost. Since then, it's been much more complicated to travel, cross borders, and converse with opposing parties. An even darker shadow was cast over Muslims and xenophobia rose from the grave if it ever had been buried. The divide between opposites has widened. Dialogue seems to be a thing of the past. In congress, members of opposing parties balk at finding compromises. Mass media has become radicalized and has opened the door to a new wave of authoritarian governments, who might seem harmless but are still authoritarian. Many imitators of Russian President Vladimir Putin have risen to power, including in the United States.

September 11th initiated a wave of attacks in many cities, including those that seemed protected against senseless acts of terror. Random explosions occurred in London, Paris, Boston, Madrid, and Barcelona, while various wars spanned deserts and swept across cities in Iraq, Iran, Syria, Palestine, Pakistan, Afghanistan, and northeastern Africa.

SEPTEMBER 11TH

The tide shudders,
retreating in all directions.
The "save yourself if you can"
of shrieking seagulls reaches land.

My kitchen also shudders
with a flurry of flour.
Muffled spoons scurry about
emptying holy vessels
and shattering pots.

The morning light shudders,
and my worn-out chair, the hearth.
The hollow shoe, orphaned
by the foot, grieves.

It was shortly after the fiestas
heralding the new century,
with promises of bread and bubbles,
and sweet delights.

It was an unexpected explosion,
treacherous, an implosion
of wings and bones, plummeting
toward the soul, apocalyptic cloud,
deluge of dark stars . . .

Even the relics
of forgotten wars
shuddered in turn.

Farewell, lost harmony,
fragile peace. In mourning,
these letters shudder and nestle
in the lap of this poem.

(From *Alfabeto de ausencias/*
Alphabet of Absences)

I seek refuge in poetry. My poems allow traces of everyday
tranquility to seep into open wounds. Is it social poetry?
I feel the urgent need to write about the horrors that sur-
rounds us. Poetry, that poor sister, literature's orphan, might

you heal painful injuries and declare with a valiant voice that the earth is wounded, and that where crystal clear waters once ran, a stream of bitterness now flows? During the summer, especially in the summer, I seek refuge in the rugged mountains. My short legs complain at times, but I carry on and embrace the breezes of the Pyrenees, where the air is still pure. I do this with the passion and persistence of a lover. I go deep into the forests in search of the peace not easily found in cities. That's where I wish to be on the final day when I'm called up. I will have left behind the pen and my poems will ensure that something remains in the memory of my children.

17

It was in the year 1959 when the regime's propaganda machinery announced with much fanfare the official visit to Spain of the popular president of the United States, Dwight D. Eisenhower, known by his familiar pseudonym Ike. For the Francoist regime and Franco, himself, it was a pivotal moment because it represented an effort to end international ostracism, both political and economic, which had been imposed by autonomous policies that questioned the legitimacy of the dictator. Would the regime have survived without that backing and vote of confidence? I'd just turned thirteen and the memory is still fresh today. I was leaving the school of Los Hermanos de las Escuelas Cristianas on Guzmán el Bueno Street when the exciting announcement, calling for a public welcome, was made on the radio and in the newspapers. Ike landed on the North American air base of Torrejón de Ardoz, a few kilometers from Madrid, where he was received with highest honors by the dictator. The procession headed for the center of the city, crossing the most iconic streets lines with nearly a half million Spaniards cheering the visitor. On the Torre de Madrid, one of the two skyscrapers that existed then, a fluorescent sign flashed with the three letters I K E, the nickname of the president of the United States, a World War II hero. It was like a massive Carnival celebration. For a kid like me, who was let out of choir practice at school, where we were rehearsing for a Gregorian mass, that event sounded particularly important. Something huge was happening. What did that visit mean for Spain? Basically, the ultimate blessing for the dictatorship, which in exchange, had to concede land where North American military bases would be installed for the exclusive use of the great power. The economic boycott would end as would the ostracism imposed by the international community. The United States, defender of democracy, sold its soul to the devil in exchange for expanding its military power in the world, thus clinching its economic power as well. On a personal level, I remember the ruckus in the streets and the exaltation in the media. I wouldn't understand, until much later, that we'd have to live sixteen more years without freedom.

With that visit, there began a period of glorification of the American nation whose economic and military resources contributed to a propaganda campaign that had global repercussions on our culture. With Eisenhower, Hollywood came to Spain with all its movie stars (Doris Day, Charleston Heston, Frank Sinatra, Jimmy Stewart, Ava Gardner, and so many others), and its singers (Elvis Presley, the Platters, Neil Sedaka, Paul Anka, etc.), not to mention the impact on television, which in Spain came slowly but surely, in black and white on two censored channels. North American culture wasn't considered subversive; on the contrary, its values aligned with Spain's ideology. The movies that came to our theaters were comedies in which tall handsome actors, wearing neckties, seduced beautiful blond actresses with long legs. They sang and danced and lured us with a happy world we wished for, with fancy houses, big cars, and daily cocktails. They represented the exuberant fantasy of post-war America. My first two youthful infatuations were with actresses who cast a romantic spell on me. The first was Romy Schneider, a German-French actress, who starred as the Empress Elizabeth of Austria, in the trilogy *Sissi*. My second infatuation was with Esther Williams, the Olympic swimmer who became an actress in films with choreographed aquatic scenes that revealed her svelte body in a bathing suit, not a bikini, which wasn't allowed in Spanish theaters. Bikinis would come much later with Brigitte Bardot, with whom platonic love transformed into sexual attraction.

Nor was I aware back then of the consequences the military agreement between Franco and Eisenhower would have. The United States, the country in which I've lived forty some years, the one I admire for so many good things, has been a military force without historical precedent throughout the twentieth century and the years to date of the twenty-first. Not one year has passed in the two centuries of its history in which North American troops have not been involved in some military conflict in some part of the planet. Its economic power is backed by that killing machine whose budgets grow whenever international politics become more unstable. It doesn't matter if the government is in the hands of democrats or republicans. The arms industry supersedes any social or humanitarian restrictions. Billions of dollars are spent on weapons that never leave the warehouses, not to mention the obsession of citizens who believe in the false notion that it's their constitutional right to bear arms. The National Rifle Association (NRA) is the organization with the largest membership in the country, more than five million members. Every time there's a mass shooting in a school or public institution, as has happened regularly for the past twenty years, the association increases its enrollment, and the sale of weapons and ammunition explodes. On one of my mother's visits to our house in Virginia, I took her to a neighborhood supermarket where you could buy things for the house, anything from detergent to bananas, coffee, cheese, and a Magnum Taurus Tracker, or a Research Desert Eagle semi-automatic pistol. All that without registering a weapon or undergoing a background check; simply step up to the cash register, pay, and go home.

My mother was totally against war or any armed conflict. That anti-war sentiment had settled in her soul after spending the best years of her youth between wars. What were her feelings? And what are mine? Ministries of War have existed for years. With the Cold War they became Ministries of Defense. Pure semantics. When I was fulfilling my obligatory military service with the Spanish army, after one of the shooting drills, they chose me to represent the army in international competitions. I have no idea how that happened. I'd never fired a weapon before. I was so horrified that I started to miss the target on purpose. I didn't want to represent anyone or have anything to do with firearms, shooting, or bullets. After living more than forty years in the USA, I still can't understand the fixation in this country with weapons.

I wonder what my father did after fleeing Madrid, while it was under Republican control, and enlisting in Franco's rebel forces? Did he carry a gun? Did he load it? Did he point it at someone? Did he shoot? At whom? I have a hard time accepting that. In the only photo the family has from that period, you can see him grinning, with a friendly smile, standing next to his brother Ignacio and an unknown soldier, as are nearly all the soldiers in times of war. Where were they going? Where had they been? When that photo was taken, which front were they on? Were they the troops on the front line or the rear guard? The Spanish Civil War was brief compared to other more recent wars, nevertheless, it was very important in a global context. The future division of the world's political and economic influence was under debate among the great powers. Fascism and Nazism were anomalies, unexpected powers that grew in the shadow of threats from labor movements and the possibility that the elite, keepers of economic power, could lose their privileges. Spain was a proving ground, a laboratory for experimenting with new weapons of destruction and assessing the resistance of its people. The war didn't solve any problem nor did World War II. The victims in Spain amounted to approximately one million, among the dead and exiled. The figures for World War II are hard to fathom. Statistics say more than forty million died, unprecedented in the history of the world. Is the world a better place after so much bloodshed? Did we create a new order that is more just? The Cold War seems to be the only legacy, an absurd confrontation as absurd as those who promoted it by selling us the threat of another confrontation. We are here and you stay there. Spain languished as a no-man's land, in a kind of limbo in which misery and the scars of war were covered up with the exaltation for a new order that embraced the words of the Falangist hymn, "face the sun with a new shirt." It's with great apprehension and a certain amount of pessimism that I write today, in the second decade of the twenty-first century, in which there's a proliferation of dictators or those cut out to be dictators. Donald Trump is its new paladin. That day in 1959, when I left school, I left ignorance behind.

18

She sits there, staring at me intently. I'm not sure if she sees me. There's the look on her face of a frightened and bewildered girl who's returned to the house where *papá* and *mamá* can't be found, just a man with a vague face, somewhat familiar but strange. I speak to her. I hold her hand and caress it. She smiles at me. She complains that the coffee, to which she's added six teaspoons of sugar, is bitter. She no longer tastes the flavors of her favorite beverage. She complains. I ask if she wants to go for a ride. She likes the idea. Going in the car is like riding on the merry-go-round at the local fair. Driving along the highway we sing "Don't believe because I sing/I have a happy heart/I'm like the nightingale/who must sing or forever depart." She enjoys the ride. For a while she escapes from her labyrinth and the anguishing confusion in her empty box of memory. When we return, she asks when I'll come back. I don't think she knows who I am. I'm the American son, the one who left and returns once a year, like the prodigal son. Her memory can't handle that many months.

Perhaps it's too soon to stop talking to you. You stopped speaking when only a hint of a broken smile crossed your lips, when that terrible dementia dragged you further and further down into deep unscented wells. You couldn't even convey the relentless pain you suffered from a malignant cancer, whose telltale sign was the bile you hurled oblivious to its source. I was the biggest coward when the decision had to be made.

When it was obvious you could no longer live alone in the house because you left the burners on and hid your treasures over and over again, treasures you never had except for the medallions of the Virgin of Lourdes, so miraculous but unable to halt your awful dementia or save the husband you prayed for so fervently. You'd put your keys in the most obscure places, and hide the few *pesetas* you had, only to turn around and search desperately with no chance of finding them. Then you'd blame the collusive act on some evil character.

Something similar happened to my grandmother Rosario, but with more vehemence. She blamed the death of her son Pepe, on a communist conspiracy when he really died from an acute peritonitis, although the truth is they let him agonize with no medical attention because it was Sunday, and the doctors were on summer vacation or moonlighting at private hospitals. My grandmother would wander the house at night on her deformed arthritic feet and spy on the *sereno*, (as they used to call the night watchman back then), convinced he was an accomplice to the conspiracy that finished off Uncle Pepe and would do away with the rest of us if she weren't vigilant. When it became obvious that my mother's neurons had been irreparably damaged by Alzheimer's, we hired a nurse to stay with her. But my mother forced her out of the house, and we had no other choice but to find a nursing home and tell her she had to leave her house, which was everything to her, perhaps all she had left. At that point, my siblings had moved away from her Carabanchel neighborhood. I wouldn't have had the courage to pack her suitcase, wrap her in her coat, and lead her to the front door for that last goodbye. I was fortunate to live far away, and it was my two brothers and sister who carried out that cruel mission.

Now it's my father-in-law who's started down that slippery slope and forgets who visited him, who called, or if he ate breakfast. He, who once was an army colonel, a lawyer, judge, Dean of the Law School, the strong man, the imposing father, now shrinks down in his wheelchair sputtering random sounds when something crosses his mind. Then he goes into a panic. This is what awaits all of us and it's not worth thinking about, or in my case, writing about. We're all going to succumb to the same pitiful circumstances. We're living longer and there must be some collateral damage to this prolongation of our existence.

19

Juan Domingo Perón returned to Argentina on July 20, 1973. Various groups and political factions who had embraced his confusing platform anticipated his arrival at the Ezeiza International Airport with lofty expectations, but his return unleashed violent confrontations that paved the way for the military coup of General Jorge Videla. This marked the beginning of one of the most tragic periods in Argentina's history, although the exodus of thousands of Argentines began in the previous decade. Many of the exiles were professionals who made a positive impact on the countries where they found refuge, while others were artists and musicians, primarily musicians. In pubs throughout major cities in Spain, you could hear their music at that time. I was especially drawn to their folkloric music. I had the good fortune to listen in Spain to Eduardo Falú, Alfredo Zitarrosa, Atahualpa Yupanqui, and other groups on tour, such as los Fronterizos, los Chalchaleros, el Cuarteto Cedrón, Jorge Cafrune, and of course, Mercedes Sosa. That marvelous Argentine musical universe from those years opened the world for me personally. Argentina coursed through my veins. Don't ask me why.

Among my mother's fantasies or memories that she struggled to remember and recount was the deep emotion she felt when she saw Carlos Gardel perform in Madrid when she was around fifteen years old. Gardel was the star of the most popular cultural export of the 1920s and 1930s, the tango. He died in a plane accident in 1935, the year before the Spanish Civil War broke out, and his death was mourned throughout the world. I don't recall my mother listening to tangos. She preferred boleros. Nor do I remember her dancing, although I have a vague recollection of her dancing the *pasodoble* at an outdoor festival. She'd sing every now and then but would stop if she thought someone was listening. Oh, her saintly modesty!

Despite all the cultural and musical influence of Argentina and Mexico on my formative years at the university, specifically la Universidad de Barcelona where I studied for five years and earned a bachelor's degree in philosophy and literature, not a single course on Latin American history was offered. But you could take courses on ancient history, modern European history, and the history of Spain from different periods, including that of Catalonia. Considering the Spanish presence in both Americas for more than five hundred years, it seems strange that in such a prestigious institution no courses on Latin American history were included in the curriculum of the history department. But that's the way it was. Perhaps that's why I felt drawn to the Americas, their geography, history, landscape, encounters, and chronicles.

It's worth mentioning that the Franco regime never anticipated the impact that universities, with their growing student population, would have as an instrument for transformation and mobilization of the opposition. My five years at the university was a period of intense political activism, participation in assemblies, strikes, and street demonstrations. Nothing of great substance, much intellectual frustration, and the desire to go to a country and attend an institution where learning was a priority. When the regime finally wised up, it was too late. One of the reasons I finally decided to emigrate to the United States was the profound feeling of futility over my time spent at a Spanish university. I asked myself, what do I know, what have I learned? What little I'd read just filled me with a sense of emptiness and helplessness. How could I go out into the world like this? I knew something about the French Revolution, about farm movements in southern Spain, about expropriation of lands and bourgeois revolutions, but little else. I was keenly aware of my deep lagoons, and it frightened me.

One of the most exciting experiences of my university years, which my meager salary allowed me to share with friends, were the trips I made to France and England. Our weekend escapes to France coincided with many festivals that turned into extended weekends. We'd travel to towns near the Catalan border, such as Perpignan and Le Boulou, among others. In those places, astute businessmen organized film festivals for Spaniards eager to see what was prohibited in Spain. The festivals lasted for days, and from early morning until late at night they'd show the best of European and American films, especially European films, primarily the most avantgarde. It was cinema that never made it to Spain because of censorship: Federico Fellini, Michelangelo Antonioni, Ingmar Bergman, Stanley Kubrick, Bernardo Bertolucci, François Truffaut, among others. They were veritable marathons in which we'd sit through five or six films in a row. We'd take advantage of those trips to buy books by forbidden authors or books on controversial topics. We'd return exhausted but feeling as if we were participants in an intellectual debate from which we'd been excluded. One time I took my mother on one of those trips to France, my prudent mother who was always anxious to please others. I don't remember everything we saw, but I do remember *Em-*

manuel, a soft porn film that was very popular at that time. She watched the entire film without saying a word, and uttered just one comment as we were leaving, "a bit strong." She was willing to put up with just about anything as long as she could travel.

It wasn't until I got to the University of Virginia that I finally encountered the history of America and began my journeys to the southern continent. I was hungry.

20

In the summers, my father took advantage of his half-day work schedule to repaint the rooms of the house. Although the furniture wasn't elegant, at least our house could shine with the cleanliness of a decent home. That's what he used to say. He took much care and pride painting our house. One summer, he was on a ladder painting the last strokes on the ceiling when he suddenly fell to the floor with a crash that resounded throughout the house. It was the first seizure and left him paralyzed on the left side. The doctor recommended a salt-free diet, which was about the only remedy for high blood pressure in those days. My mother ordered loaves of bread without salt from the neighborhood bakery, and we all followed the same diet. Fish without salt, lettuce, and garbanzos as well. It was the summer of 1956. There was no Lipitor or other effective drugs, and so the family turned to the saints for a miracle and made promises to the Virgin Mary. There was talk of taking him to the sanctuary of the Virgin of Lourdes in southern France or to the one to Fátima in Portugal, but we had neither money nor means for that. My Uncle Paco, a sergeant in the Civil Guard, offered to make the trip and returned with water from the fountain of Lourdes, blessed and miraculous water, and a few medallions. It came in small bottles that he'd take sips from daily. He could barely manage to make his way to the neighborhood church of Cristo de la Victoria to pray the rosary and who knows what else. All to no avail.

In the school of Los Hermanos de la Salle, where we studied, we'd take part in every one of the many religious festivals, each with a dramatic staging. Perhaps those scenes are part of the Catholic rituals that stayed with me. During Lent we'd read passages from the Bible about the arrest, torture, and crucifixion of Jesus. We'd read aloud perched on a church pew. I must've recited well because they cast me in one of the roles. I liked it. Also, during Lent, but mainly during Holy Week, they staged the Stations of the Cross, which recreated the journey of Christ to Mount Calvary or Golgotha. They erected fourteen stations that commemorated the tragic moments before the crucifixion. At school, they prepared us well in advance for this period of sadness and sacrifice. During those weeks we couldn't eat meat on Fridays and had to deprive ourselves of things we craved or loved so that we could appreciate the suffering of the Son of God.

One afternoon, when they'd described to us in detail His suffering on the cross, my emotions, fear, and youthful passion made me think I should experience the pain myself. I needed to experience it first-hand. And so, when I got home, I took a hammer and a long nail from my grandfather's toolbox. I went to my room and placed the nail on the palm of my hand and gave myself a weak blow that was forceful enough to pierce the skin and leave a red mark. What religion would have us suffer such pain? Frustrated by my masochistic failure, I decided to try something else, if only as a symbolic gesture. So, this time I took a safety pin from my mother's sewing box, closed my eyes, gritted my teeth, and stuck it through my earlobe. The pain was imperceptible but fulfilled its function, my share of sacrifice.

They were somber customs that concurred with the ideology of the Franco regime. Had it not turned Spain into a country of mourning with an unjustified and fratricidal war? Wasn't it for the best to believe we deserved so much pain because of our liberal, communist, and atheist ideas? Isn't it true the dictator slept in his bedroom with the virtuous arm of Santa Teresa watching over him? Did he not call for celebration while soldiers who fought in the war were still being pursued and imprisoned, along with members of the younger generation who protested the national mourning and raised their voices demanding freedom? My father, a devout Catholic and to a certain point Francoist, never recovered from the embolism. It has taken us decades to recover from those sad and pious practices. Many believe that Francoism continues to have lasting effects on Spain in the twenty-first century.

21

I write from the Chesapeake Bay, on the east coast of the country, where I've spent more than forty years. This surprises my Spanish friends who ask me if I like living in the United States. My answer is simple: I don't live in the United States, I live in the University of Virginia, which my dear friend Evangelina Rodríguez Cuadros, Professor at the Universidad de Valencia, describes as an Arcadia. Other friends of mine who've spent time in Charlottesville, such as Juan Martínez-León and his wife Cristina Domenech, feel the same way. The America that seduced me is the America of great explorers, those who traveled to the Caribbean or the Chesapeake Bay where they encountered a totally foreign world with societies well adapted to their environments, but light years from the achievements of the European Renaissance. They say this continent has been inhabited for fourteen thousand years. Adventurers and people in search of land began to cross the Bering Strait and eventually made their way through deserts, plains, coasts, and jungles to the southernmost tip of the continent. They settled along coastlines and lakes, and lit fires to keep warm. Those flames dotted the landscape, which is why travelers to that remote region gave it the name Tierra del Fuego.

In some way, I too am an emigrant. I left Castile first and then Catalonia to settle in the Appalachian Mountains, where in 1891 Thomas Jefferson laid the first stone for the foundation of the University of Virginia. The university has been a protective mother who opened her arms and libraries to me and taught me to read with discipline and a critical eye. She surrounded me with colleagues and professors whom I admired and who showed me how to pursue an intellectual life and explore the world through books that spark the imagination. I truly admire my North American colleagues who are passionate about other languages and cultures, and there are many of them. Colleagues of mine, such as David T. Gies, a professor and specialist in romantic theater, loves everything Spanish more than any of my friends born in the Spanish peninsula. He loves its cities, streets, literature, cinema, and theater, perhaps because he's so familiar with them. You could say he's a dreamer. I can say the same about Carrie who, after a trip to Israel for an archeological dig, ended up in Spain, and ever since has dedicated her career to studying its cultures, fiestas, and people with sincere passion and a sharp critical perspective. I wonder if I feel the same way about America. Perhaps I do, or maybe I'm just a poor idealist in search of my other half.

After settling in Virginia in 1978, we took trips out west in our Chevy station wagon, crossing the Mississippi River, backbone of the nation that separates two coasts, and venturing into the plains of the Midwest and the Rocky Mountains. We visited national parks and saw the many wonders of this land, before finally reaching the Pacific, where in 1804 Lewis and Clark revealed to the United States the geographic treasures of the nation. Theirs was the first voyage that North American citizens had ever made from coast to coast. It's true others had visited those coasts before the expeditions of Lewis and Clark, such as Hernán Cortés in the sixteenth century, or Juan Rodríguez de Cabrillo, who reached the San Francisco Bay in 1542. During all my American adventures,

I thought how much I wished my father could've shared the journeys with me, but he died when I was just a boy. I still remember his broad forehead and green eyes, and his hearty laugh that rose from his chest with joyful sincerity. Perhaps I'm a bit obsessed and he's perfectly fine wherever he is.

While pursuing the master's and doctorate, my studies prompted me to retrace the routes of explorers, and for emotional reasons I can't explain, drew me by chance to America, especially to Argentina. The destinies of those poor dispossessed farmers, soldiers, and artisans who embarked on ships and sailed the sinister seas to unknown coasts intrigued me. They landed on beaches with manatees and alligators, or ended up in the jungles of the gulf, where they came across pyramids erected by cultures as ancient as their own. I tried to understand the resilience of those adventurous soldiers who, in search of a better life for themselves and their families, enlisted in expeditions to who knows where. They marched thousands of kilometers from the archeological remains of Teotihuacán to the northern plateaus where Pueblo Indians had constructed cities of wood and adobe. They made their way to many places, although in their minds and recollections they'd discovered nothing worth noting, except for their tales of the massive herds of bison they saw, those venerable beasts that roamed the plains and made the earth tremble under their hooves.

Both my master's thesis and doctoral dissertation focused on Argentine history: journalism in the nineteenth century and the dictatorship of Juan Manuel de Rosas, one of history's villains. I was interested in Argentina's myths and legendary figures, especially its nineteenth century explorers and nation builders, and the first emigrants. I studied the works of the Mansilla siblings, Lucio and Eduarda, as well as its early literature, especially the accounts of *cautivos*, captured women and men. I've dedicated a great part of my scholarly endeavors investigating all these topics with what some would consider a rather abnormal passion.

It was through my friendship with Mempo Giardinelli, whom I met in Virginia, that I became familiar with Buenos Aires and the rest of the country. Mempo welcomed me into his home with open arms and that broad sincere smile of his, the sign of an exceptional person. Mempo is one of the most impressive Argentine writers of the past four decades. He's the author of dozens of books of essays, short stories, and novels, including *Santo oficio de la memoria*, a fascinating novel about an Italian family that emigrated to Argentina. But more importantly, he's a socially engaged man who believes each of us is responsible for what happens in this world and is convinced that our actions are not useless acts but have direction and purpose. His commitment to cultural and political journalism stems from this conviction. His primary goal and motivation are to create a nation of readers. He views reading as an intimate, reflective, and intellectual act that rescues us from the dark circle of ignorance and provides a broader perspective of the fascinating world around us.

Mempo represents Argentina, open, extensive, embracing. He greets you with a bear hug, wide, tight, and broad, like his body. His features, like Argentina, are seductive. Few people I know have such a contagious laugh and mischievous and penetrating gaze. He speaks with the passion of lovers, although his words reflect a sense of logic and ethics. I've crossed the Argentine landscape numerous times with him on trips to Mesopotamia and the northern provinces of Jujuy, Salta, and Santiago del Estero. In the north he reported on the train stations that were left abandoned because of the privatization of railway companies by corrupt governments, at that time, the presidency of Carlos Menem. On another one of our journeys, we traveled south from the Chaco province, where Mempo resides, following the majestic Paraná that becomes even wider as it joins other rivers that empty into the Mar Dulce and finally into the maternal waters of the Atlantic. The rivers of America are grand, nothing like our streams in Spain. After reaching Mar del Plata, we continued our journey along the coast until we crossed the invisible border into Patagonia, where we were greeted by the statue of Ceferino Namuncurá, son of Manuel Namuncurá, and grandson of Juan Calfucurá, one of the last Mapuche chiefs of the territories that border the valleys of the Andes and the plains of the Pampas. Ceferino Namuncurá witnessed the end of the period of constant conflicts between the original Indigenous tribes and those who wished to expand the Argentine frontier.

On this six-week journey, we spoke and listened to many people, and opened up to one another with the respect of two people who truly care deeply for each other. We took walks, climbed hills and mountains, and wrote. Mempo is a professional writer and needs to write to be at peace with himself. Writing is his vocation and civic responsibility. During the journey, he sent brief chronicles to a Uruguayan newspaper that were later published in a fascinating book, *Final de novela en Patagonia*, which is comprised of observations made by a traveler in his own homeland, a country of myths and legends. In this book, Mempo combines the diary of a journey with reflections on literature and elements of fiction, all woven together in a surprising but coherent text. Meanwhile, I took my time composing a volume of poetry, something of a testimony of my impressions of amazing glaciers and the solitude of savage nature.

PATAGONIAN PATHS

Roads leading nowhere.
No crossroads in sight.
Rosary of stones
over scars pierced by
the savage afternoon wind,
at the hour guanacos woo.

Today is today and yesterday gone,
without a doubt, languishing savanna,
traversed by ñandus and stars.
Bones charred
by the relentless rule
of the sun over its creatures,
the shadowy ones and the somber beings,
those parched with thirst and the others,
those pale daughters
of the ice who keep its secrets.

Along came a man, a woman,
the first steps of the tenacious sandal
planting a whirl of furrows
over the land that opened
like a womb in labor, under
the daily grind of toiling heels
in their obsessive quest to find
nothing, the hidden face of the south,
the elusive City of the Caesars.

And Route 40 wound its way there,
unheralded beneath feet that harvested dust.

(From *Anotado al margen. Cuaderno de ruta/
Marginal Notes. Road Notebook*)

When two people of the same age (we were over fifty then)
and sex travel together for forty consecutive days and the
journey transpires in harmony, without arguments, it's because the friendship is solidified.

In the year 2000, when our trip took place, Patagonia
was still a pristine space untouched by the maleficent imprint humans tend to leave behind. You must gaze on the
gravel roads, the *páramos* dotted with wild plants, and the blue-
green waters of lakes fed by glaciers to appreciate its history.
Stones could narrate the adventures of the Telhuelches in
their hunt for *guanacos* and *ñandús*. For several centuries,
that copper-skinned tribe managed to avoid the sway of vis-
itors to their land (Magallanes, FitzRoy, Darwin, and Meth-
odists) until the republic buried them like a tombstone. The
nations of Chile and Argentina competed to raise their flags
over their villages and hearts. They failed to do so, but along
the way the number of victims grew. Later, the deplorable
actions that culminated in the slaughter of rural workers,
described in Osvaldo Bayer's novel *La Patagonia rebelde* (*Rebellion in Patagonia,*) extended the reach of the paternal embrace that civilization bestowed upon all corners of the land,
even the most remote.

During our journey, we shared our reflections on literature, history, and politics. Mempo commented on the ap-
athy and disorganization of local governments responsible
for meeting the basic needs of the population. One example

is their unwillingness to promote and preserve the natural beauty of the region. There's some truth to the adage that Argentina is *el culo del mundo*, the asshole of the world. Just turn the map of the Americas upside down and move the north to the south, and it's as if Argentina's destiny could be altered in that one subversive act.

I've returned to Argentina every year since my first trip in the 1990s. I search in the archives of Buenos Aires and other provincial capitals for information about captives, for a tiny stray piece of fabric that tells the tale of that woman and that man whose story has yet to be told, while it lies within the pages of a dusty manuscript in the historical archives of a local city. I've been invited to many barbecues and shared good wine from Mendoza and lively conversation with people and cultivated many friendships. I've read my poems at numerous events and in theaters of provincial cities and have felt poetry spread its wings and find its humble way into the hearts of those listening, just as I hoped it would. I wonder about the essence of poetry. It doesn't sell or make its practitioners famous. Nor does it heal wounds, create wealth, or pass judgement. But one verse of a poem is enough to stir emotions. In the advanced stages of the Alzheimer's that consumed her, my mother, who couldn't remember her name or distinguish the flavor of foods, could recite poetry. We'd get her started with a verse and she'd spill out the rest as if it were tucked away in some drawer or box of her confused mind, lying silently dormant.

In the city of Resistencia, capital of the Chaco province, where I stay when I travel to Argentina, there's a bar, a kind of local bohemian spot called *El Fogón de los Arrieros* (The Hearth of the Mule Drivers), where they hold a *milonga* once a week. Tango lovers meet up there, those who dance and those who sing, while others sit at a table with a bottle of Malbec watching the interlacing steps of the dancers and listening to the hoarse voices of the singers. I like to go to that special place. I don't dance or sing tangos, although I'd like to. I've tried out a few steps now and then. They know me and on more than one occasion have asked me to recite poetry. "Let the Gallego recite," they cry out. I don't make them beg and recite García Lorca's "*Prendimiento y muerte de Antoñito el Camborio camino de Sevilla,*" "*Romance sonámbulo,*" or a sonnet from the *Sonetos del amor oscuro.* I'm amazed by the admiration that García Lorca evokes in that city of Italian and Spanish immigrants, Toba Indians, and residents of the northeastern Chaco province. What is the magic of poetry? What is the seductive power of the land?

22

In 2018, Spain celebrated the one-hundred-year anniversary of the Ordesa y Monte Perdido National Park. It was King Alfonso XIII who inaugurated Spain's first national park in 1918. I was in Ordesa with my friend Vicente, loyal escort of my annual retreats to the Pyrenees, and companion of other adventures. I made my first trip to the Pyrenees when I turned eighteen. Few emotions are as intense as those you have when climbing a mountain. The first visit was a rite of initiation that transformed me. Ever since, I've returned faithfully to renew my vows and commitment to nature. For years, I scaled the mountains of Guadarrama and La Pedriza. I wasn't good at it because of my lack of technical training, but I forged ahead without thinking about it, like I do so many things. Every time I found myself dangling by a rope against the stone face of a peak, I'd asked myself what was I doing there. Fear took hold of me. I put myself at great risk because of my lack of technical preparation. Perhaps that's why I'd return week after week ready to confront a new challenge. Isn't that the way life is?

My passions are related in some way to my experiences in the mountains. Even my early religious period had its beginning there, sitting around campfires in the countryside at night. You feel so insignificant, but at the same time such a part of nature that your emotions rise to the surface. Climbing La Faja de las Flores in Ordesa that summer of 2018, I reaffirmed those deep feelings were still alive and patted myself on the back. As a boy, my most remote adventure consisted of going with my parents to where the Manzanares River flows by El Pardo, about fourteen kilometers from Madrid. El Pardo is a town north of the city, where Francisco Franco made a home for himself in what was once a hunting lodge built by King Enrique de Castilla in 1406. Carlos V transformed it into a palace in 1547, and in the 17th century it was remodeled by the architect Francesco Sabatino. The palace and town are surrounded by mountains that overlook the town and hunting reserve where the dictator shot deer and wild boars. In the palace, which was off limits back then but now open to the public, you can visit the private chambers, including the bedroom where next to his bed and kneeler, the dictator kept the virtuous arm of Santa Teresa de Jesús, or so they say. It seems rather medieval. What did he pray for? To what God? To what higher power did he appeal to carry out such a bloody war? Who named him the chosen one? The 50 pesetas coin was engraved with his image and these words: "Francisco Franco, Leader of Spain by the Grace of God." Did he assign that epithet to himself, or did someone convince him to embrace that destiny?

On a mountaintop sits the Iglesia de la Virgen del Carmen de El Pardo, the church inaugurated by the dictator in 1966, and the convent of the Sisters of the Immaculate Conception. Inside the church, a glass case displays the figure of a suffering Christ in agony. The imagery of the Catholic Church is particularly bloody and funereal. On a recent visit to Spain, I took my grandchildren, Ryder, Lulu, and Austen who were then six, five, and three years old, respectively, to see several churches and cathedrals in Segovia and Ávila. Standing before the images of a crucified or wounded Christ, tortured martyrs, and sorrowful mothers, their infantile minds begged an explanation. Who could help me tell a five-year-old girl that God the Father sent his Son to be sacrificed for the redemption of our sins? What exactly is the redemption for suffering? What virtue does it have? I'm reminded of these verses by Blas de Otero: "I wish to find, I go around searching for the causes of suffering, of suffering for its own sake." My explanations sounded to them and to myself like a surrealist tale. Is the sacrifice of the Son of God what attracts people to Christianity? Fortunately, neither the Valley of Ordesa nor the mountains of my sierras or other ranges have anything to do with a bleeding Christ. The mountains are pristine, the perfect expression of nature, without guilt or punishment.

This summer, I had the chance to return to Benasque, a very charming town, typical of those in the Pyrenees. It was a ritual of return of the prodigal son to its rivers, peaks, and landscapes: Batisielles, la Renclusa, el Perdiguero, el Posets, la Besurta, and El Refugio de Estós. My friend Chad and I wanted to climb the Aneto once again, but the hot temperatures made the ascent difficult. The snowfield, known as the Aneto Glacier, was melting at a rapid rate, which complicated our climb. Our feet sunk into the ground and rocks emerged sharp as blades. It's normal for steep ascents to be challenging for mountain climbers, but what's not normal is for the temperature to soar to 95 degrees, in the Pyrenees, in the month of June, making the expansive glaciers start to disappear at the same rate we count the passing years and the wear and tear on our legs. It's not a matter of talking about the potential global warming of the planet and what we can do about it. What truly matters is understanding that this planet and its natural wonders are all we have, and they belong to all of us. For this reason, taking care of them is our collective responsibility.

23

I went through my hippie stage. In the sixties and seventies, revolutionary movements advocated enticing calls for sexual, political, and social liberation. They championed freedom from the repressive teachings of the church and from constraining social and political doctrines, regardless of their origin or affiliation. After breaking away from my Christian phase, I needed to recover from the rupture of my first marriage, which had been a hard blow. So, I went off to Barcelona with little more than a few books and records. It was time to start over. Like the poet Antonio Machado, I was never political, nor does revolutionary Jacobin blood flow through my veins. There's something conservative in my nature that stems from the Operé side of the family and restrains my fainthearted revolutionary actions.

My sexual revolution amounted to trying to convince the young university coeds I met that making love solely for the pleasure of the body was a healthy act of rebellion, but these attempts met with little success. I did participate, with some reluctance, in activities organized by a few clandestine groups, such as street protests and other demonstrations against the government, but I did so primarily because it was expected of university students during that tumultuous time. I also tried to break from family and cultural traditions. I rejected my religious beliefs and even thought about stealing an album or food from the supermarket to test myself. To be honest, it was simple opportunism on my part.

On our required reading list were books on Marxism inspiring us to create a socialist society. During the first elections in Spain in 1977, I voted for the Communist Party, which in Catalonia garnered 17% at the ballot box. With time, my revolutionary adventures waned. From the Communist Party, I went on to vote for the Spanish Socialist Workers' Party (PSOE). Who knows how my political affiliations will develop. We become more tolerant with age, don't we?

What other acts of liberation formed part of my private revolution? Every morning, from my house in Barcelona's Floresta neighborhood, where I lived with Carrie, I'd go to the shop around the corner and buy croissants for breakfast and the newspaper. Upon my return, Carrie would ask, "what's new?" For nearly two years my response was the same, "Franco has died." Was that my only act of defiance? Finally, after repeating it so often, on November 20, 1975, desire became reality. Franco died. On that day and those that followed, the streets in the area were littered with empty champagne bottles. We needed to build a democracy, but with no previous experience, we didn't know how. Democracy's a difficult and risky exercise. Of the approximately 190 countries with established governments in the world, only nineteen have fully functional democracies. The threat from powerful authoritarians is constant. They pursue relentlessly, ready to overturn fragile democratic institutions. Even in the United States, one of the oldest and most stable democracies is faltering under current proceedings and practices. As I write this now, during Trump's administration, when I come home and Carrie asks if there's anything new to report, my response is *ojalá*, I wish.

After the death of the dictator in Spain, the threats to the fledgling democracy became real. The Basque terrorist organization known as ETA, which had been praised for being one of the few opposing forces against the excesses of the dictatorship, turned into a repressive apparatus that ignored democratic norms and laws in pursuit of its political objectives. They operated clandestinely, using weapons to kill without warning and exploding car bombs that triggered the mechanisms of terror. Threats and attacks cropped up all over the peninsula. The Basque province of Euskadi suffered the consequences of ETA's campaign to liberate the region from the supposed yoke of Spain. Its citizens were the first victims and paid with their own blood the repercussions of that homicidal scourge. ETA used a narrow criterion to decide who were friends and who were enemies. My dear friend Germán Yanke, an open-minded intellectual and an honest and fair man like few I know, was on their blacklist for a while. He'd been the director of Bilbao's Centro Cultural Miguel de Unamuno, which was named after the highly respected intellectual and writer of the Generation of 1898 who advocated for a rebirth of Spain stemming from Castile. Because Unamuno didn't favor regional demands for independence, the left-wing Basque Nationalists considered him a contemptible figure.

On a recent trip to Bilbao, I encountered a city that had recovered its exuberance. During the transition period to democracy, while ETA decided if it was time to abandon arms, the Basque region endured a long black night during which any deviation or disagreement with their criminal policies could be considered a direct threat. Brothers no longer confided in sisters. The enemy could be the butcher or the baker, as Fernando Aramburu narrates so well in his novel *Patria*. What tragic harm was committed by those sick individuals who drank the tonic of extorsion and fear while deciding the destiny of others without respect for freedom of thought. After the death of Franco, the Spanish people embraced social and political freedom, even while fearing the return of a dictator and his henchmen and while suffering the anguishing threat of terrorism disguised as national liberation.

24

My initial North American experience wasn't easy, just the opposite. I was driven by a desire to study in a university where
learning and research were a priority. I didn't speak English
and could barely mutter a few sentences I'd learned in a two-
week summer course in England, and from a few other classes.
I hadn't considered all the obstacles I'd encounter, and they
nearly defeated me. I came to the United States without having read the brochures or weighing the difficulties I'd face. My
knowledge of the country was based on movies I'd seen, west-
erns, the happy-go-lucky world of Frank Sinatra and Doris
Day, and hundreds of films shot in New York City. Carrie and
I ended up in the heart of America, on a farm surrounded by
hills, woods, and deer, fifteen miles from the small university
town of Charlottesville. On the other side of the road leading
to our prefabricated rural house was a country store that sold
gas, tobacco, and some basic goods. Arnold, the owner, spoke
an Appalachian English that even locals from the city couldn't
understand. He seemed to speak without opening his lips, letting his sentences slip between his teeth. I struggled with the
language, the solitude, the constant rain, and the desire to
return to Spain as soon as I finished my studies, which I hadn't
even started. It was a way of living in the future and avoid-
ing the present. A kind of limbo in a no man's land teeming
with troubles. We planted a garden whose abundant harvest
became a burden. We didn't know what to do with so many
tomatoes and cucumbers.

I wrote letters constantly, mailing them like messages in a bottle cast into the sea in hopes of a friendly response. My mother wrote back with maternal promptness. Many years later, after she died, I recovered all the letters I'd sent her, and was surprised by what I'd written. Soon after settling in Virginia, Philip was born, as beautiful as the rising sun. But his light wasn't enough to lift my spirits. Each day, I climbed the hills around our farm and walked through the woods trying to replicate my hikes in my sister Sierra, the Guadarrama mountain range. I played the guitar and sang in local bars to help make ends meet, but those experiences depressed me even more. Can you imagine a bearded Spanish immigrant, sitting on a stool in the lobby of the Holiday Inn, or in a Mexican restaurant, singing Spanish ballads and the occasional bizarre version of an Argentine *milonga*? And to cap it off, I don't play guitar well. I can only strum a tune and not much more. Once I was hired to sing in a Japanese restaurant, the Four Seasons Steak House, where waitresses from El Salvador and Mexico dressed as geishas and bowed their heads as they tried to play the part. Meanwhile, I sang my heart out from a little platform. What an extravagant example of globalization. Another time, I got a gig at a golf club and the owner made me go around the tables playing guitar and singing with a certain Latin flair. The final straw was when he suggested I perform in the club's restaurant dressed as a bullfighter.

After a year as a farmer and extemporaneous singer, I was about to throw in the towel. I was allergic to the constant pollen of springtime in Virginia. Its rainy mountains were not suited for light-footed hikes like those in the mountains back home. The benevolent solitude of the farm become an asphyxiating prison cell, so I returned to Spain for the Christmas holidays. Shortly after arriving in Madrid, I climbed the Guadarrama mountains in search of my roots and crossed the terrain during a heavy snowstorm. Then I traveled to Barcelona to try to recapture the emotions of my college years. But the problem was me, not Virginia. I realized I had to pay the dues that America and the American experience demanded of me. And that's what I did. I returned in January 1980 eager to change assumptions based on past experiences. The key was finding harmony between body and mind. It's not possible to live in a place physically while constantly thinking about another. I stopped writing letters so frequently and going to the mailbox anxious to find a letter from a friend. I stopped reading newspapers from Spain that eventually made their way to the university library. I listened to NPR news programs on the radio and watched broadcasts on TV and became a fan of NBA basketball and American football. With the help of a couple enthusiastic friends, we organized the first soccer league for adults. I donned my soccer shoes and started to play and enjoy the present moment as much as possible. My son, born in 1978, had turned two, and it was time to be a father, something I hadn't done with my daughter Marta. She stayed in Spain when we moved to Virginia, and I've always missed her.

25

It's hard for me to pin down the when and where of most decisions I've made in my life. That I was born in the Argüelles neighborhood of Madrid and studied in a Catholic school seems certain. That my father died when I was twelve years old, certain as well. There's evidence of those events, and I was there and suffered. At some point, I don't know when, I realized I should accept my uncertain and dreary future. They took me out school when I was fourteen and put me to work a few weeks before my fourteenth birthday. It donned on me then, like a flash of lightning, that the only way to escape my bleak destiny was through education. I asked my mother to find a school that offered night classes so I could continue my studies. After several years, I enrolled in the university and took all kinds of classes, from humanities to the social sciences. I could've studied psychology, sociology, art history, economics, anthropology, and history, although theater was the greatest draw for me. I don't know where that passion comes from, certainly not my family. I ended up earning a bachelor's degree in history and literature. Before leaving for the States, I applied to the Department of Media Studies of a few North American universities with very demanding requirements. It was the time when the TV and film industry was expanding, and it seemed a good option for me. I wasn't accepted at any of them, although I did receive a scholarship from Smith College in Massachusetts to enroll in a graduate program for American Studies. After visiting the campus in February, in the winter when the snow was more than three feet high, I thought snow was fine, but not so much. Then we decided to stay in Virginia where Carrie had begun her doctoral studies in anthropology. I tried to make similar arrangements in the Department of History, and enrolled in their program for Latin American history, of which I knew nothing except that Columbus had arrived at the continent in 1492. The rest was nebulous. Now, forty years later, I'm a professor at that same university, perhaps because of another concatenation of coincidences.

I've written several books; more than I'd ever thought I'd write. I'm not sure if I'm a researcher at heart, but at least I'm not a bookworm. Maybe it was the environment and witnessing the academic pressures on my colleagues that lead me down that path. If circumstances had lined up differently, perhaps I would've continued as the director of the school of business I helped to start in Barcelona. Going down a different road, I could've had a career as a B-list actor in low budget films or acted in a provincial theater. I could've devoted my career to therapy and psychoanalysis, like my dear friend Antonio Soler, my roommate in Barcelona, or my brother Mariano. But no, I took classes on Latin American history and literature at the university founded by Thomas Jefferson in Charlottesville. I love the profession. I also remember my aspirations to become an expert mountain guide and how I spent every weekend and even Christmas vacations climbing mountains in my teenage years. For some of these vocations, I had no talent or experience. For others, I counted on what was most essential, the power of desire, which has probably been my main weapon, transforming certain aspirations into passions. Where does that come from? Were my parents passionate about learning or did they concentrate on getting through each difficult day during the war and afterwards. Were their lives a constant struggle between nonconformity and dreams? And my Sevillian grandmother, the one who stands by me when I need her, what did she rebel against? What I ask of life in these years of perpetual sunsets is that desire remain, and death catch up with me while I'm pursing impossible ventures.

My father was a great reader, although I can't remember exactly what he read. He loved poetry and could recite fragments of poems by Bécquer and Machado. During the years he was sick and wasting away before his death, he used to read the book of meditations by Thomas Kempis, *De la imitación de Cristo*, in a pocket edition he carried with him, and the Bible, whose beautiful mythic texts have been used and abused by some Christians throughout history. My mother read anything she could get her hands on, or that we recommended. When my brothers and I were little, my sister would read the stories of *Antoñita la fantástica* outloud to us, and we'd recite children's stories that we'd memorized. As an adult, she loved historical novels. My brother Mariano, an inquisitive intellectual, reads everything he can and should, especially the works of the classic Spanish poets San Juan de la Cruz, Quevedo, and Góngora, but always he returns to the *Quijote* and repeats passages from it. My brother José Luis is a fan of detective and crime fiction. Sitting on someone's lap, we heard the sermon on reading.

What would my life have been like without books? Since childhood, my access to education wasn't easy. The economic woes of the family that required me to work eight hours a day, kept me from being a full-time student. I had to fit my studies around my work schedule, not to mention other distractions of my youth, such as playing guitar, acting in plays, mountain climbing, or falling in love like a fool, a beautiful pastime at seventeen years of age. Reading is what saved me from an abnormal education. It was through books that I learned to train my sensibility, explore language, question undeniable truths, and attempt to emerge from a fog of ignorance. To go through life without discovering something about the world in which we live, even a fraction of it, seems a sad proposition. And so, I devoured books with the passion of an argonaut. I read in bed, on the bus, in the park, at the dentist's office, walking down alleys or wide avenues, on the summit of Mulhacén mountain, or lying on the beach on a sweltering day. I must confess that I've forgotten nearly all or almost all of what I've read. If only a tiny fraction remained in my memory, I'd be an erudite expert, which I'm not. What passes through my eyes fades like a sliver of light through a window blind, but the emotional component remains in a beehive of thoughts accumulated over time. The facts have vanished, but those thoughts form the ideological framework of my intellectual being. And so, despite my faulty understanding, weak retention, and deteriorating memory, I'm conscious of the universe in which I live, its historical periods, and the place on this planet I've had the good fortune to share.

Everyone knows, but denies,
their last exile.
They also recall exact days
of birth, a certain evening,
the cross above the church.

They say, "I was born,"
"I went to school,"

"I fell in love."
They say it daily,
without a fuss,
just like that.

They call themselves
Pedro, Andrés, Cecilia, Rosa.
They hang on to memories
that hurt deeply or delight,
and display with zeal
their most intimate treasures.

And God? Who does he marry?
With whom does he share his silence?
Does he write, perhaps,
the encyclopedia of the world?
Does he determine births, decide dates
of demise, find unity
in opposites?

Meanwhile, we carry on
amid enigmas and high
intentions. We amuse ourselves
celebrating the end of the year,
the happy birthday,
the weddings of Canaan,
the morning full of grace
that isn't ours
but has white wings,
resounding innocence,
ringing like a belltower.

Because I was born one raucous day
of October that I don't recall.
I buried my father
and donned sadness for a cap.
I loved a blond-haired girl
 and was stricken by memories.
I prayed to deaf ears
and meditated. Ruminating,
I remained entangled in a
labyrinth of loves and dates,
mysteries waiting
to meet their match.

That I was born one day,
is a fact. That I'll die
slowly, is a grave matter.
That I'll leave without answers,
I have a feeling I will.
Let's rejoice, then, to the end,
my friends,
and live for the moment.

(From *Salmos de la material
Psalms of Matter*)

26

The more you try to recall certain events, the more blurred they become, teetering on that fine line between memory and fantasy. When I was eighteen, the religious organization I belonged to appointed me to a leadership position that promoted cultural and sports activities for youth groups. One summer, they put me in charge of selecting camping sites for our weekend outings. For some reason I can't explain, I decided we should spend the weekend in the Sierra del Ocejón, northeast of Madrid, a mountainous area no one had explored previously, and no one in the organization was familiar with. Least of all me. As the supposed leader, I decided we'd go there in the month of July of 1965, as I recall. The date is approximate, as are the memories of what happened. I vaguely remember that two buses with 120 young hikers pulled into a parking lot of a town, perhaps Tamajón or Valverde de los Arroyos. We got off the buses without the slightest idea of our location. Without asking a local, I pointed towards the mountains that surrounded us and we began climbing in that direction. We finally made it to a flat area half-way up the slope and I decided we should camp there. There was no water or sign of a stream around there. I was so thirsty I opened a can of artichokes and drank the liquid. The next morning, I sent squadrons to search for water and a path to reach the summit of Ocejón, situated at an altitude of 6700 feet. I just learned this figure now on the internet, as I write this. I went off on my own to achieve both objectives. After hiking several miles, I came to a tall cliff with a mighty waterfall cascading over it. I stripped, and let the water drench me as in a baptismal rite and drank until I quenched my thirst. There's always been an element of luck in my life, a guardian angel, or an unexpected turn of events that comforts or guides me. I don't mind being alone. I've hiked alone many times in the mountains. I believe I reached the summit of Ocejón. After midday, I decided to return the same way I'd come in the morning. In my foggy memory sketches of an arid landscape appear. Suddenly, halfway down the trail, I heard the strumming of guitars. Where could that music be coming from? Also, voices singing. It seemed strange in that wild place to hear someone singing Andalusian tunes. Today I'd say the situation resembled an Iberian version of magical realism. Did it really happen? Soon, a group of young men appeared out of nowhere playing guitars and belting out *alegrías*, *bulerías*, and *sevillanas* on their way down. It was one of the squadrons and among them was my brother Mariano who, at that time, was into flamenco and often went to the Casa de Córdoba in Madrid.

Fortunately, on that calamitous weekend in the mountains of Ocejón, we didn't lose anyone, which could've easily happened. There were no accidents, which would've been normal, and no one became dehydrated, also to be expected. And all because of the irresponsibility, or better said, the adventurous spirit of their leader, me. Has this been the tendency all my life? He who takes no risks doesn't cross the sea. This is literally true, I can confirm it, or maybe not, perhaps there's another way to sail or live, something I'll recount in the next round.

27

When our kids were in high school and turned sixteen, we had to buy them a car. In the United States, if you have no means of transportation, you're either dead or useless. The lack of public transportation makes getting around difficult. The cars we bought were used, but at least they ran. Our second son, Peter, didn't settle for just any make and searched the market for a second-hand car worthy of his self-image. He put himself in charge of the mission and somehow managed to get us to buy him a Saab, and later, a Volvo. He totaled both in accidents. Fortunately, he wasn't injured, but we had to attend traffic school as punishment for our irresponsible son. It was a way of penalizing the parents.

My father never had a car, nor did he learn to drive. The same for my mother. My father liked to tell us how his boss would sometimes bring him home in his car, describing with pride their journey through the streets of Madrid as if it were a grand adventure. In the fifties and sixties, practically no cars existed in Spain, except for a few private automobiles and taxis. We lived on Guzmán el Bueno Street, on the corner of Joaquín María López, in a middle-class neighborhood close to the center of the city. In the afternoon, we used to play soccer in the street. The metal door of a shop served as the goal and took a beating from all the balls we kicked at it. Now and then, the game would be interrupted by the shouts of "car," and we'd pause to let it go by and then continue playing.

In those days, people got around by trolley, metro, and bus. We rarely took a taxi, and walked everywhere, from one neighborhood to the next to visit aunts and uncles and other relatives. When my father suffered his first stroke, his left arm and leg remained partially paralyzed. After months of slow recovery, he still had a noticeable limp but insisted on returning to work. He didn't want to sit around all day in an easy chair feeling worthless. My mother would help him get dressed, open the front door for him, and send him off with a kiss. Then she'd follow him from a distance, keeping an eye on his frail body until he disappeared at the entry of the first metro station. That was ten blocks from the house. She'd follow him into the metro too and board the next car without him seeing her. When it arrived at his stop, she'd watch with a protective gaze, until he made his way to the entrance of the Platería Espuñes company. Then she'd return home and, in the afternoon, repeat the same routine so she'd be waiting for him when he left the building. Once she got closer to our house, she'd hurry ahead and enter through one of the large patio windows, put on her apron, open the front door with a smile, and ask, how was your day? The afternoon hours slipped away between dinner and our playful ruckus. He was on his way home from the church of Cristo de la Victoria when he suffered his final stroke, and a good Samaritan lifted him from the sidewalk and brought him to the house in a taxi. Out of curiosity, while writing this episode, I googled Platería Espuñes and read that it was a factory that made silver objects, founded in 1840, by Ramón Espuñes. The factory had its own pavilion in the Iberoamerican Exposition held in Sevilla in 1929.

My first car was a Simca 1000, which I drove like a maniac through the streets of Madrid as If I were racing on a motor speedway. I should've been fined heavily for such reckless driving. The car belonged to the father of my girlfriend, but he never drove it because he didn't have a license. I suppose he bought it as a status symbol. Shortly afterwards, he sold it, and I bought a Renault 4x4, with four-wheel drive, which seemed like a luxury to me. I wasn't as crazy with that car, because for one thing, it never reached cruising speed and it made such a racket you couldn't even listen to music on the radio. The history of cars is like that of girlfriends, in my case, few and far between. I sometimes joke with my bachelor brothers that I was born married or engaged. They've somehow managed to wriggle out of commitments.

I use my bicycle to get to many places in Charlottesville. I own two cars, but only need one. The bicycle relieves me of a certain sense of guilt I feel for the excessive use of automobiles whose exhaust eats away at buildings and facades like termites and contaminates the air. How's it possible that air pollution continues to blacken windows and the lungs of city dwellers? Did my father live a more restricted existence because he never had a car or driver's license, and took La Veloz bus whenever he needed to take a trip? He never flew in a plane or crossed the sea in a boat. His short legs were those of a walker, like mine, and his shoulders were sturdy and his forehead broad. Was he happy? Does happiness have tangible and ethical components? Is happiness impartial or is it simply the body's reaction to feeling content? I always had the impression my father was happy despite his worries, a man with few aspirations whose life revolved around his wife and children. Perhaps the dismal time in which he lived made him the man he was, or maybe it was his upbringing in a small town surrounded by olive groves, horses, mules, and hunting dogs.

28

The name of my school was, and still is, San Rafael. It was one of the schools los Hermanos de La Salle ran for children with limited financial resources. There were others in Madrid for students of upper-class families who paid tuition for their children's education. My school was free, but getting accepted was a challenge. Because it was free, it only offered a general education. The curriculum consisted of basic studies, particularly courses, such as accounting, to prepare students for the labor force. They also offered courses in the humanities, including history, religion, languages, composition, drawing, music, and poetry. An annual poetry competition was held in that school for children with limited financial means. They encouraged us to memorize a poem to recite in our classroom. Then three students were selected from each class to compete in the final contest, which took place in the auditorium with all the students and teachers present. There were three categories of winners: emperor, king, and prince. It was quite the honor to win one of these distinctions, which was rewarded with a trip to the Sierra de Madrid at the end of the school year.

Admission to the school wasn't easy because it was free of charge. I don't know what the requirements were. They made me take an entrance exam, which I failed, but my father managed to tip the scale in my favor with his charming personality. I performed well in the poetry contests, but never earned the distinction of emperor. I couldn't finish the last year of the five they offered. A few weeks before I turned fourteen, they took me out of school and put me to work so I could contribute to the dwindling household finances. And so, I parachuted from the childhood games at school to the depraved maneuvers of the business world. I found myself in a perverse and selfish world of mediocrity that had no appeal, where the struggle to get ahead was the norm and the rule. Between my half-finished schooling and my premature entrance into the labor force at the age of fourteen, I kept one foot in adolescence and the other in the adult struggle for survival. I tried to stay clear of those cynical losers who were incapable of dealing with their dark feelings. What stands out from those nebulous years is my autodidactic drive for knowledge. I read novels when I was just a boy. I became a member of El Círculo de Lectores, a reading club sponsored by a publishing house that mailed books on a regular basis. I'd request recommended novels or those that seemed intriguing to me. That's how I came to read *In Search of Lost Time,* that marvelous novel by Marcel Proust, possibly one of the authors who's most influenced me. Also, Graham Greene, Pío Baroja, Azorín, Stendhal, and everything that fell into my hands. Perhaps reading those books opened my eyes, awakened hidden desires, and ignited my tendency to join associations or groups that had something to offer, no matter what, but something. I wanted to follow in the footsteps of those adventurous literary heroes.

29

Shortly after moving to Barcelona, my childhood friend Alberto decided to move to England. He ended up in London and wrote to me about the freedom he was discovering in that society, so seductive and fascinating, according to him. Both of us had been educated in religious schools and by Jesuit organizations. The impact of religion marks you for life, for one thing because of its mythical nature, and for another, its strong commitment to austerity, responsibility, and social engagement. It has a little bit of everything. Some of them positive aspects of Christian Humanism. In London, Alberto had decided to come out of the closet, as they say nowadays, and give absolute free rein to his homosexuality. He invited me several times to visit him and I finally did with a few classmates from the university. We drove directly from Barcelona to London without stopping, twenty straight hours crossing France and reaching Paris in the morning.

To us, London seemed an alluring and unique city, different from others we'd seen. We marveled at neighborhoods with their row homes, each with tiny gardens and short staircases to the front door, where fresh bottles of milk were deposited in the mornings. Those neighborhoods with their tree-lined streets and gothic cemeteries seemed straight out of a fairy tale to me. Everything was foreign but charming. Alberto welcomed us and introduced us to friends in the gay community where he lived. Besides eating fish and chips every day and corn flakes for breakfast, the greatest novelty was drugs. I discovered in London that the rule of thumb was to live on the edge. The new creed called for its followers to break norms for the sake of breaking them, give in to a world of intoxicating stimulants, raze the barriers between the sexes, renounce guilt and sin, knock heroes off their pedestals, push aside myths, dismantle legends, violate certain behaviors, and enter forbidden spaces. On the surface that ideology sounded appealing, but it couldn't be carried out for lack of a sustainable theoretical foundation. That's what happened to most of the revolutionary movements in the seventies. Lots of rock, nudity, and drugs, a lot of drugs, strikes, and protests against wars, efforts that slowly lost steam the older we got. But in the meantime, dreams lived on.

From the start, England stood out as the country to emulate. How could we use it as a model of freedom and tolerance for Spain? The first steps we took back then were to overstep the limits so we could free ourselves of inhibitions, as Alberto had done. Unfortunately, drugs are false inhibitors. They keep you in an illusory state that might be pleasant for a few moments but are deceptive in the long run. Don't misunderstand me, I'm not trying to pass judgment. But to be honest, the world has suffered tragedies for decades because of drugs, but far be it from me to wave a magic wand and solve the problem. I just wanted to share what I finally came to understand years later after trying LSD, marihuana, and hashish, which is that true liberation stems from knowledge and stimulating intellectual and physical adventure. Alberto returned years later, after coming out, having many lovers and some painful relationships, and following the gospel of pleasure without limits. He stayed at my house, and we enjoyed our close friendship while he was still here. Sadly, he was among the first victims of AIDS, when the disease came into the world as an epidemic that would end humanity and its excesses.

England continues to be part of my life in several ways. My daughter Camila married a true Englishman, Adam, whose personality and accent evoke the British Isles and remind me of that country I admired so much in my university days. Our niece Maggie also married an Englishman named Lee. After their father's death, Carrie and her sister Molly decided to research the origins of the Douglass family in Scotland. To that end, we've taken trips in search of ruined castles, following the trail of traditional ballads whose lyrics tell the bloody history of confrontations. As I write this chapter, the Brits have decided to cut ties with Europe in pursuit of the imperial dream they once lived, as if history could repeat itself. It seems we're living another epoch of separatism and disagreement. Globalization turned upside down.

30

When I finished college, I traveled throughout Europe (France, Greece, Italy, and Portugal), and in 1974, I went to the United States, the place that would end up being my home for more than forty years. I'd met Carrie in Barcelona and thought she was the most beautiful woman I'd ever seen, tall and blond, with an air about her that reminded me of the Hollywood stars I adored as a teenager growing up in a backward Spain. There she stood before me and miraculously took an interest in me. She agreed to go with me to a jazz festival in the Palau de la Música in Barcelona, and to the music of Charles Mingus, Thelonious Monk, and Miles Davis, we began to form a relationship based on true communication, mutual trust, and shared passions and interests. I invited her to take a weekend trip to Pedraforca, a small town in Catalonia, at the foothills of the Pyrenees, an invitation she accepted provided I have a seatbelt installed in my Renault 4x4. I had to ask a mechanic I knew to add straps, or something that resembled a seatbelt, at a time when vehicles left the factory without that safety feature. There followed a series of amorous encounters that culminated in a trip to Texas, where her parents lived. We flew to Boston and from there began a road trip, a la Jack Kerouac, of more than forty hours to Houston, the city erected beneath the shadow of petroleum. Houston is a metropolis that suffers from the most undesirable aspects of contemporary culture. A city without an urban plan and streets without sidewalks. A city with big cars, and multiple freeways dotted with criss-crossing overpasses. A city in which the rights of the individual come before those of the community, in other words, the essence of predatory capitalist individualism.

Back then, as our Greyhound bus descended the highways of the Eastern coast, I wasn't aware we were headed into the heart of America, the Bible Belt, which embraced slavery and fought on the side of the Confederacy during the American Civil War. That war left indelible scars, some of which have yet to heal. The so-called Jim Crow Laws, enacted by white state legislators after abolition, were responsible for reproducing a system of segregation that lasted another hundred years and whose consequences are still felt today. Racism continues, although tempered. Every now and then violent protests by white supremacists arise, like the one that took place in my city of Charlottesville, in August of 2017, with a nod of approval by President Trump.

The bus made stops in Manhattan, Charlottesville, Atlanta, and New Orleans. We spent the night in each of these cities and made passionate love, as if it were our last night together, like the lyrics of a bolero. Who would've told me we'd spend the next forty years in the city of Charlottesville, home of the University of Virginia? In my office at the university, I keep a photo that my brother Mariano took of us posing on campus. Carrie's wearing bellbottoms and a loose flowered blouse, and I'm sporting a thick beard with hair down to my shoulders. Two hippies. Carrie is now a professor of anthropology, and I'm a professor of literature and Latin American history, in the very place where that snapshot was taken. It moves me deeply when I think of the ways life offers itself to us. I say life and think of destiny, luck, chance, providence, and coincidence. Perhaps it's also energy, willpower, chemistry, and enthusiasm.

Hey life! Does no one respond?
Words go round and round; flashes of lightning recorded
in years that were once stone and today are mist.
Life never responds.
It has no ears, it does not hear us;
it does not speak to us, it has no tongue.
It does not go or stay:
We are the ones who speak,
we are the ones who go on
as we hear echo after echo and year after year
our words tumbling through a tunnel without end.

(From Octavio Paz "Respuesta y reconciliación"/
"Response and Reconciliation")

In Texas, I learned so many things I never knew. The population of Houston is 40% Mexican. The majority are immigrants who crossed the border in recent years in substantial numbers. Texas gained its independence from Mexico in 1838 and joined the United State in 1845. The new settlers grabbed the land and its riches and displaced the original Mexican population and the Indigenous (primarily Apache and Comanche) communities. Today it's difficult to foresee in which direction that complicated social balance will lean. What I do know is that at first, I felt estranged from both communities, the Mexican and the Anglo. That's where I met John Jay Douglass, my future father-in-law, a person who had a great influence on my life. He was an upright, confident, and fair man, and an indefatigable traveler with a strong commitment to family, which he handed down to his children, thus creating an extensive family that he watched over like a truly generous and kind patriarch. When I visited Houston for the first time, we ate lunch in a typical Texan restaurant that served barbecue and lots of beer. My future father-in-law insisted on accompanying me to the restroom out of fear someone would take me for a Mexican and cause trouble for me. Back then, I wasn't aware of that underlying racism. Now I am. The United States is a strange country in that sense. Racial and cultural tensions have more presence than in other nations of the Americas, even in countries where the mixing of races has always existed, with slavery as a contributing factor. I know of no other country with more religious, ethnic, and linguistic diversity. The American melting pot is presented as a false myth, but the border with Mexico has been and continues to be a source of conflicts.

SOUTHERN BLACK MAN

Mouths of hunger,
eyes of fire,
muddled in the night,
asleep in their own cemeteries.

Southern Black man, black silence,
nostalgic strains
resound in a clamor
of drums and saxophones
from an ebony heart.

Gazing down
you call upon the heavens
and there goes your soul
shimmering like a star.

Gleaming teeth
and lips in flight,
muscles ready
to sidestep fear.

I've seen you in the south
on plantations of dead slaves,
gathering debris,
raking in time,
burrowing in the white world
your age-old scorn.

White world of whites,
bitty ramshackle house,
where the moon darkens
the cotton-picking bones.

Bodies tired
of saving skin,
Black man from a Black history
darned by decrees.

(From *Alfabeto de ausencias/
Alphabet of Absences*)

After that trip, I began to explore the Americas, driven
by all that was new to me and my academic career as
an historian. I've traveled both Americas from north to
south, like the first explorers, from Francisco de Orellana
to Vázquez de Coronado, and from Jiménez de Quesada to
Hernando de Soto. I've visited their cities, spoken with their
people, and listened to them, traversed their land, taking in

all there was to see. My scholarly books, volumes of poetry, and my American consciousness were born from those trips and explorations.

31

If anything has been a constant in my life, it's my love, my passionate almost desperate love for literature: poetry, novels, theater, and film. They've entertained me, fulfilled my fantasies, inspired my journeys, and filled the hours of my day. Through my readings, I've learned about human nature in all its splendor and misery, for which I'm truly indebted. I remember so many books, like great loves that left their mark on me, books I can't forget that captivated and seduced me, filled my days with light and questions, with emotions and ideas. Certain books have such an impact that closing them when sleep overcomes us seems a betrayal. You'd like those books to never end, to keep spinning their tales forever. I'll name a few that fascinated me and remain vivid in my memory, although there are so many, the list would be endless: *The Quijote* by Miguel de Cervantes, *La Regenta* by Leopoldo Alas Clarín, *Sor Juana Inés de la Cruz or the Traps of Faith* by Octavio Paz, *The Name of the Rose* by Umberto Eco, *Patria* by Fernando Aramburu, *The War of the End of the World* by Mario Vargas Llosa, *One Hundred Years of Solitude* by Gabriel García Márquez, *The Burning Plain* by Juan Rulfo, *A Heart So White* by Javier Marías, *Diamond Square* by Mercé Rodoreda, *The Man Who Loved Dogs* by Leonardo Padura, *The Metamorphosis* by Franz Kafka, *Absalom, Absalom!* by William Faulkner, and *Soldiers of Salamis* by Javier Cercas. As for poetry, those writers who've impacted my work, and whose books of poems are my perennial favorites include San Juan de la Cruz, Francisco de Quevedo, Antonio Machado, Miguel Hernández, Federico García Lorca, Pablo Neruda, Walt Whitman, Emily Dickinson, Charles Simic, Blas de Otero, Juan Gelman, César Vallejo, Nicolás Guillén, César Simón, José Martí, Jorge Luis Borges, and José Emilio Pacheco, among many others.

LIBRARY

The man saw tomes stacked like tiles,
cliffs of books in a row,
and emotion washed over him.

His entire being, what he once read and forgot,
and the little he remembers, all gathered there.
He gazed and his mind conjured
a universe of stanzas,
the first notebook,
the book that beguiled him,
evoking joy and heartache,
when he was still a virgin of words,
unable to string together a sentence.
He felt at peace in that sacred place
assembled with centuries of legends,
stories, and poetry.
And he recalled Cortázar,
Machado, Walt Whitman,
and the voice of his father
in whose lap he heard the very first tale.

(From *La imprudencia de vivir/
The Recklessness of Living*)

Lately, I wake up at night after sleeping two or three hours at a time. What would seem a problem whose only solution is a sleeping pill, has turned into pleasure. During those periods of insomnia, I read novels, many novels, tons of novels. And I love it, especially because during the day I read for my research and academic work. Alberto Manguel writes that "reading is one of the most delicate forms of adultery." For Antonio Muñoz Molina, "reading is the only sovereign act we have left." Francis de Croisset once wrote that "reading is the journey for those who can't take the train." All these statements sound good, but what's certain is I love to be told stories, read them, think about them, and let my imagination fly in the space of fantasy and ideas that is literature. Perhaps it's like returning to my mother's arm, when as a little boy, while sitting next to her or walking beside her to some place, she'd tell us familiar stories, embellishing them as she went along, stories she remembered, or the plot of the last movie she'd seen. I'd cling to her lap and let her tale seep inside me until I identified with the characters, good or bad, who belonged to another universe beyond the world in which I lived.

32

My employment history reads like a farce. Fabra y Coats, the textile company where I worked for seven years was a silent witness to my years of frustration, although not wasted years. I look back on that time and it seems a century ago. Life's never squandered, even though it seems that way. You always get something out of an experience, whether it's good or bad. I didn't learn much in that company, except for certain underhanded tactics employed for survival. I finally got a better paying job at a publishing house for books and medical journals. They hired me to publicize a horror magazine, actually a comic book series. Maybe the culture wasn't ready for that genre like it is today when horror films are box office hits. No one supervised me and I didn't have a clue what to do. I lasted only four months until they kicked me to the street for absolute incompetence. Through a dear old friend, I got a job that very day with SEAT (Sociedad Española de Automóviles de Turismo), the first Spanish car manufacturer. My work was a torturous bore lacking any incentive. I spent eight hours a day looking at the clock, trying to make the daily nightmare pass quickly. I searched for another job and landed one as the administrative director of a branch of the Margaret Astor cosmetic firm. I was put in charge of accounting, with the disadvantage of not knowing a thing about accounting. I've never shrunk from a challenge. Luckily for me, one of the women in the office realized my predicament and helped me keep the books up to date. Until one day the inevitable occurred. The branch manager had his own furniture business and didn't trust his accountant. So, he brought me the ledgers and told me to look them over and let him know if he was being ripped off. I took the financial documents home and put them on a table, glancing at them from time to time and waiting for a voice or a red flag to signal fraudulent activity among all those figures. I returned on Monday, and with the documents under my arm, entered the manager's office, and confessed, much to his surprise, that I hadn't found a thing because basically I knew nothing about accounting. I was fired on the spot. That situation, combined with the failure of my first marriage, prompted me to pack my few belongings and move to Barcelona to escape my professional and romantic failures and find something better. Shortly after, I got a job at an advertising firm that lasted a little more than a year. They found out I'd been teaching classes at a middle school in the afternoons, and given I'd signed an exclusive contract for my measly salary, I was fired. Quite the winning streak! In a short period of time, I managed to get kicked out of three companies. A brilliant professional career did not seem promising. Maybe that's the way it is for nearly everyone when they first start working, especially those of us who begin at the bottom. Or maybe I wasn't cut out for administration. Perhaps destiny had a more favorable adventure in store for me. When she learned about my abrupt exit to Barcelona, my marital separation, and my multiple employment disasters, my mother cried. My mother always cried; that was her mighty weapon. She never confronted her sons, but one of her tears was more powerful than any exhortation.

33

Soon after celebrating our wedding day, my young bride was diagnosed with tuberculosis. Her primary physician recommended total bed rest, or sitting in a chair, until her lungs cleared up. Weren't there antibiotics? I remember it all like a nightmare, a blur of anguish and waiting rooms for days on end. A friend, there's always a friend, recommended we visit a specialist whose experimental treatment hadn't yet been approved by health institutions. We asked for an appointment. The idea of keeping a patient who just turned twenty in bed for months seemed like absolute torture. The doctor prescribed medicine that he himself produced in his private laboratories and gave her permission to walk and lead a semi-normal life, even swim, everything in moderation. He thought it wasn't a bad idea to spend time in the mountains.

World War II brought with it an epidemic of tuberculosis. Soldiers who returned from the front came back vomiting blood. The illness weakened them slowly but surely until they were walking skeletons. Penicillin wasn't widely available then. The first experiments date back to 1941, but its commercialization didn't come until decades later. Before that, they built tuberculosis sanitariums in mountainous areas. Several were built in the Sierra de Guadarrama, a mountain range between Madrid and Segovia. There weren't many cures at that time, but they believed fresh mountain air could combat the illness. The ruins of those sanitariums still stand in the mountain pass of El León and la Barranca de Navacerrada.

Another friend recommended we move to the mountain village of Lozoya. They let us stay in the parish house that the town's priest kept as a second residence. It was a stone house that faced the church. The idea was for us to stay there until my wife recovered. We passed time bathing in Lozoya's fresh spring waters and taking walks to the river. I'd get up early in the morning to buy a loaf of bread, hot from the bakery oven, a fleeting pleasure of rural life. At midday, I'd cook something for both of us and we'd read in the afternoons and listen to music. The Beatles had just separated, and Paul McCartney had put out his first album as a solo artist. Solitude seeped through the stone walls and our spirits. The complications and suffering succeeded in creating a distance between us that became a wasteland. I spent my vacation with her, but when summer ended, I had to go back to work. I'd travel back and forth to the city, while her sister and mother took my place. Miraculously, the unauthorized doctor's treatment worked, and, in a few months, my young wife improved physically, but her soul was shrouded in a dark cloak that brought on a crisis it's best not to talk about. That story is hers alone.

They were difficult years. It's hard to comprehend illness and death, especially at a young age. She was twenty when her body suffered the devastation of illness and psychological crisis. My father was forty-two when he suffered his first stroke, and forty-four, when he died. Before that, he enjoyed sweet years with his family, strong and healthy children, a loving wife, and a job. He shared his good nature with a close-knit group of friends and family. I don't know what dreams he had, or plans for the next forty years, which naturally should have been his to live. He had a strong body and good habits. He never drank, but he did smoke. His passions were soccer and nature, and we often spent time outdoors. He loved his wife with devotion and his children were chicks born under his wings. The grim reaper came with his scythe and took him away. I remember the feeling I had when I turned that same age, forty-four. I was twelve the year he died, and my son Philip had just turned that same age when I celebrated my forty fourth birthday. Pure coincidence. Life has granted me thirty more. I hope it gives me a few extra. We'll see how long this story can last. Now that I've forgotten how to pray, I pledge vows to the planet.

Death is a great mystery and the only irrefutable presence. As a kid, I earned a few pesetas in the neighborhood parish serving as an altar boy. Not only did I assist with the Sunday mass, but I also sung in the Saturday service, and accompanied the priest who was sent to bless the bodies of the deceased before the burial. Back then, there were no funeral homes like in the United States. The dead lay at rest in their homes, where they received the final visit of family and friends before being taken to the cemetery. They used to hire professional mourners to weep, which must've been emotional or terrifying, but that was before my time. I've always loved dramatic enactments. The priest would hover over the body, ready to bestow the pious blessing to the dead soul with oil and holy water before their final journey. I'd be there, wearing my altar boy tunic and carrying the pail of holy water, while assisting in that mournful event with a watchful eye. Maybe I got used to it. In a brief period, after losing my father, several other family members passed away: my Uncle Pepe, my Aunt Pepa, my Uncle Antonio, my Uncle Paco and Aunt Elvira, and my grandparents, Antonio and Rosario. We had to touch them, kiss them on the forehead, an icy cold forehead. I was afraid to do it, but we had to. Today they're present in the photos of a family album, which with help from modern camaras, we can now digitalize to prolong their memory. I don't know if my children have any interest in those photos I show them from time to time, or if they'll even be interested in this story I write, which stirs up emotions with surprising intensity.

34

After working six years in an antiquated company founded in the 19th century, a tiny light went off in my head. It was that flame, the kind that glows inside and sheds light on an uncertain future. "Where will the road lead?" asks Antonio Machado. The one I was on didn't seem to be going anywhere. I spent my days working, six days a week, from 8:30 in the morning until 6:00 in the afternoon, and on Saturdays until 1:30. I whiled away the late afternoons courting early romantic prospects on long sunset walks in El Parque del Oeste, stopping behind one tree or another for furtive kisses. On Sunday afternoons, I'd go to a *guateque*, what we called the impromptu dances held in someone's house. Not much more than that. Was this how the years would go by, languishing in a stream of mediocre monotony?

I asked my mother to find a night school where I could continue, or better said, begin my high school studies. The light shone on a distant and uncertain future, but at least there was a glimmer of light, which convinced me that education was the only way out of darkness. Neither of my parents went to college. Their youth had been interrupted by the Civil War, World War II, and the mandatory military service for males following the war. Nevertheless, my mother drilled this message into our heads: "education is the lifesaver." And it was. I enrolled in a school run by the Jesuits, which offered night classes from 7 to 10 in the evening. With my work and class schedules, I had to find time to study by sleeping less or while commuting. Madrid is a city with great distances between one place and another. I soon realized I could walk and study at the same time and get a good workout to boot. I'd often walk from my house to work, from work to my house for the lunch break (the day was split into two shifts), from work to school, and finally from school to home at night. At least I burned many calories, and that molded me into the person I am, a walker. I took advantage of the routes to read or look over class notes. I kept that routine for five years until I began my university studies at la Universidad Complutense de Madrid. I studied there for a year until I decided, for sentimental and other reasons, that it was time to break free from Madrid and move to Barcelona in search of something different, a fresh start.

During the years of night school, I was drawn to nature and religion. Although I'd attended Catholic school since I was five, religion hadn't had an impact on me. I was familiar with Christian rites and doctrines, and prayers in Spanish and Latin, and I'd assisted with mass as an altar boy and sung in the church choir for many religious services. Even with all that, religion was more of a cultural obligation than a belief. My parents were practicing Catholics. Religious images and statues hung on the walls of our house. Everywhere in Spain, festivals and holidays revolve around the calendar of saints' days. To me, those celebrations seemed a natural part of the local customs and traditions passed down for generations. The exception for me was Holy Week, whose dramatic spectacles provoked anguishing concerns over divine eternity.

The academic center, where I attended night school, was part of an organization called *Hogar del Empleado*, whose mission was to offer a humanist education to young workers.

To that end, they organized trips to the mountains of Madrid and Ávila, believing that contact with nature and disciplined participation in organized sports would contribute to a healthy education. Sitting around the campfire on Saturday nights, we'd discuss our place on earth from a Christian perspective. We celebrated mass in the fresh mountain air and took communion before setting out to climb the tallest peaks. The mystic aspect of camping in the mountains hails from military, falangist and Jesuit influences. Juan Ignacio de Loyola, the founder of the Jesuit order, was a soldier. The Spanish Falange was modeled after Italian fascist squadrons. To be honest, the impact of nature shook my emotions to the core, and the forests and mountains entered my life along with the Christian God in an undeniable and personal way. Christians refer to that belief as faith. And so, I had faith and took communion following the Christian principles of this world and the great beyond. Ironically, it was those same Jesuit priests who opened my eyes to the political situation in Spain and the injustice of the dictatorship. They were young, enthusiastic intellectuals inspired by the new doctrines espoused by Pope John XXIII, and the *Pacem in terris* encyclical he issued, whose impact was felt by Christians around the world. What's amazing is how quickly I went from Christian mysticism to communist evangelism. In fact, the two have much in common, especially the evangelical movements embraced by the poor and liberation theology. I traversed the mountains of Guadarrama, which today is the National Park of the Sierra de Guadarrama, exploring its trails, cliffs, crags, peaks, meadows, and woods. The mountains remain part of my life. They never change; I do.

In my twenties, God exited my life much quicker than he'd entered it. One morning I woke up and all that remained was the memory and incomprehension of a few beliefs picked up along the way. My religious studies led me to reject religion, and have made me more critical, even more negative, although I still recognize its positive aspects, which it truly has. The history of religions and their battles form a tragic script. In the words of Javier Herrero, my mentor at the University of Virginia and a great scholar who after retiring dedicated himself to studying the Bible, "the more I study it, the less I believe."

35

As I write, the Spanish Congress has approved the exhumation of the remains of the dictator Francisco Franco, who died in 1975 and was buried in a crypt in El Valle de los Caídos that he had built for himself like the pharaohs of ancient Egypt. Perhaps this act of justice will serve to erase the memory of those deplorable years still present in the collective memory. I'm amazed by the careless and frivolous way the liberal right treats historical memory. Franco not only presided over authoritarian governments but was the general who led a coup that cast aside all principles of democracy. He launched a fratricidal war, followed by years of repression that awakened demons in the Spanish people. Franco wished to enlighten the country, and under his orders, troops executed thousands of Republicans without due process, bombarded cities systematically, ruined the economy, which returned to autocratic mercantilism, and suppressed with one fell swoop all the social and educational advances that the Second Republic had implemented. Women returned to subjugation by their husbands and lost their freedoms, education fell once again into the mellifluent hands of the Catholic Church, the rich got richer, and the postwar regime, with its capital punishment and vicious prisons, did away with a million Spaniards who were murdered or disappeared. The senseless assassination of Federico García Lorca, who was killed without a trial on the side of a road between the towns of Víznar and Alfacar, would be evidence enough to show the magnitude of the loss. García

Lorca, the greatest poet of the 20th century, was assassinated at the age of thirty-eight. He had at least forty more years of endless creativity left in him. They killed our poet and robbed us of him. The war left us like abandoned orphans, stripped of our art and artists. It was a crime against humanity and the punishment should have been doled out to the executioner. But that's not what happened. The executioner was buried with highest honors and his body still receives prayers from those who visit his tomb. García Lorca was a universal poet, but it was forbidden to read his works and celebrate him, as if his ghost could rise from his anonymous grave and threaten the fragile peace the dictator maintained with salutations and parades. Last May, I participated in the Poetry Festival of Granada, and my friends, Fernando Valverde and Nieves García Prados, who organized the event, took me to the road between Víznar and Alfacar, where, in some ditch, between the soil and its roots, lie the remains of the poet. And now they say the remains of the dictator shouldn't be exhumed? What kind of a country is this that still preserves a monument of gigantic proportions in honor of his memory?

On a school trip I took as a boy to the monument of El Valle de los Caídos, the bus stopped near the site where construction was taking place. To our childish eyes, it seemed as if out of the rocks rose a hand with huge fingers in whose palms we could seek refuge. The hands were hoisted to the top of the monument, visible from all the towns in the valley. They were the fingers of the apostles whose statues would surround the cross. Democracy returned after Franco's death and Spain exercised its right to join the European institutions, threatened today by a new inflexible right-wing order. Dear travelers of the 21st century, let's not allow ourselves to be fooled by deceitful lures.

36

Shortly after arriving in Barcelona, Antonio Matamala and Elena, two friends I knew growing up in Madrid, took me in. They were psychologists and lived in a one-bedroom apartment with a small living room, where I slept on the couch, and a tiny kitchen. That's where I debuted my skills as a cook. Hanging on the kitchen wall was a ham, a gift from their parents. I'd look at it and my mouth would water. They barely touched it, and it bothered me to think that ham would go to waste hanging on the wall like fodder for flies. At night, I'd get up and sneak over and cut off two or three strips that tasted divine and curbed my incessant hunger. Those pleasant months helped to heal some of my wounds. On weekends, we'd go to a beach on the coast, packing a pressure cooker with a prepared meal inside, and a pile of books to read. Always, even now, I get the feeling I must catch up on my education, as if I must recover the years I lost when they made me work full-time. Later, I sublet an attic with beautiful views of the city rooftops. It had no hot water and I had to take a cold shower every morning, proof of my capacity for sacrifice and strong will. I compare those years with today's Spain, with its intense process of modernization, and can't believe the conditions under which we lived back then. We had no telephone or television, only a portable radio for listening to music while doing household chores. I love to iron and have a knack for cooking. There were no computers or internet back then either. My entire graduate career, I typed all my papers, exams, and the theses for my master and doctoral degrees on a Hispano-Olivetti typewriter. Each correction or revision from my directors meant I had to retype twenty to forty pages. My parents didn't own a Hispano-Olivetti, or an electric razor, mixer, or vacuum cleaner. It was the reign of manual things: paper and pencil, straight blade razor and frying pan, fire and burner, and clothes hung to dry outside on a line. My mother cooked over charcoal. My father listened to soccer matches on the only radio in the house, and on Tuesdays, the family would gather to let imagination run wild while we listened to the weekly melodramas broadcast on the radio.

My question is, were we happy? Memories fade with childhood and only a few remain vivid. Images become blurred like slides projected one after the other. I see a hallway, coats hanging on a hallstand, a room with a window looking out on the yard, rain forming puddles, a cold cup of coffee on the table, a Three Kings cake, the long wait for their arrival, a pile of gifts, and much more, everything mixed and confused. Swirling amidst those fuzzy images is a feeling of peace and tenderness. Maybe I had a happy childhood. If I did, I owe my overall tranquil disposition to it. I like to think this is so because happiness abides in me, or perhaps it's the serotonin in my body that produces that miraculous effect. Many things make me sad: wars, orphanhood, injustice, segregation of all kinds, poverty, illness, and a long list of etcetera's. I don't think sadness is a negative condition because it can be beneficial if used for positive change. It's a feeling that doesn't falter because something inside keeps it steady. For the most part, I enjoy bursts of intense optimism without knowing where they come from. Is it a chemical equilibrium? Happiness comes down to feeling pleasant sensations, no matter their origin, or how irrational they may seem. In other words, everything depends on our biochemical equilibrium. But aside from individual happiness, we must remember we're not alone in this world. For this reason, I believe in humankind and our capacity to do good. I believe in creativity, even though it's in constant conflict with destruction, like two opposing forces in a philosophical duel.

After living in the attic on Aribáu Street, I rented an apartment with three friends: Antonio Soler, an old friend of mine from Madrid who was a psychologist and exceptional intellectual, César el Tete Borri, a Catalan friend whose wife kicked him out, a ball of chaotic and rowdy energy, and Malene Bally, a French woman who moved from London. Her soul was in constant search, and I loved her a lot. We were like a family, sharing our space, clothes, games, food, laughter, and trips to the beach and the mountains. It lasted as long as all good things last, a blink of the eye. The place was crowded with girlfriends and lovers, and intimacy evaporated, but, as the song goes, *"que me quiten lo bailao,"* "you can't take that away from me." Barcelona ushered in years of searching and growth.

> To someone who lent me an ear,
> I confessed my fear of dying
> before the debut of my first spring.
> How could I amend
> the blank pages of monotony?
> Through my native hypotenuse
> a ravenous wind howled,
> sending me off to Barcelona
> in hopes of salvaging
> a handful of esteem.

I discovered the pristine light of the sea
and gems dreaming beneath its waters.
Her lofty beauty took me in,
gave me bread, and opened the door
to life's chaotic ambrosia.

Beloved shadow,
radiant smile
of a mystical encounter.

How quickly time passes
when you don't keep an eye on it.
Along the Ramblas
I sought bosoms of love
and sketched beaches and shores.
I read Espriu as puffs of steam
pushed a train up the Tibidabo.

I forged friendships in plazas and alleys
to the rhythm of the sea
abandoned in winter.
Before a magical Gaudí
I listened to the sermon of the wind
and bought a one-way ticket
for the next day.
My companions were
a bannerless San Jordi
and the spiraling light waving
over his shoulders.

I don't know if the first storms
have passed, but under the flameless color

of the ancient Mediterranean,
Barcelona rises in my memory,
amid Roman walls
and Greek causeways, and a dragon
who praises in Catalan the salt of the port
and its bloody emblems soaked
in the saliva of silence.

There I wrote the first chapter
of this long saga,
disguised as a poet.

(De *Ciudades de tiza. Paisajes de papel/*
Chalk Cities. Paper Landscapes)

While studying in Barcelona at the university for five years, I travelled through Europe, and pushed the legal envelope in so many situations. I fell in love again, one, two, three times, in a mad rush, and paved the way for the next chapter of my biography, which I remember now as a fusion of liberation and nostalgia. The Barcelona I knew, from 1971 to 1978, was a city revitalized by the energy of freedom and a fledgling democracy. In the final years of Franco's power, you could sense the regime was wounded and nearing the end, although Spaniards never killed the father and the dictator was buried after an agonizingly long illness and laid to rest under a gravestone that weighed several tons, in case he tried to rise again. The partying, carousing, and the time of excesses known as *la movida*, came later. There was no sector of society that didn't feel shaken by that tsunami of liberation. All limits or prohibitions were considered a remnant of authoritarianism and therefore rejected. Sexuality exploded and explicit sex was portrayed in all Spanish films. Churches weren't profaned as they had been during the Republic Period and the Civil War, but they were abandoned. Legal acceptance of drugs led to rampant and wide-spread consumption. I don't know how much of that liberation was purely cosmetic. There are many who insist today that elite falangists still hold power disguised under the cloak of democracy.

37

As a boy, I spent summers with my grandmother in Peña Grande, back when it was a neighborhood or small town with little working-class houses on the outskirts of Madrid. To cope with the sizzling afternoons, we'd walk to the Manzanares River, a few kilometers away, or I'd entertain myself hunting little lizards. One day, I started to make a fire with straw and branches, and it took off. The flames reached the nearby wheat field and wiped it out in no time. I hid under my grandparents' bed, not daring to show my face, while my grandmother apologized to the owner. I don't know what agreement they made, or if my grandmother had to pay him back. I doubt if she did because she had no money to spare. At times, she'd take me to one of the nearby movie theaters in Madrid to escape the summer heat. To get there, we'd take a trolley that dropped us off in Cuatro Caminos, a crowded working-class neighborhood bustling with markets that sold, among other unusual things, whale meat that my grandmother would cook in tomato sauce. Maybe because I was always hungry or wasn't so particular about what I ate, that whale dish tasted delicious to me. She also cooked pig's feet, guts, lots of hearts and livers, intestines, and chitterlings. I couldn't tell you what those last things were. In addition to a market and shops, there were two movie theaters on the main plaza of Cuatro Caminos, the Metropolitano and the Montija. The latter was a kind of hole-in-the-wall place where the unemployed spent afternoons and couples went to make out.

Summers are scorching in Madrid and people sought refuge in movie theaters that were always packed with all sorts of individuals, from the unemployed to retired folks. Before playing the double feature, they'd show a newsreel called the NODO (acronym for *Noticieros y Documentales*, Newscasts and Documentaries). Without TV sets at home, the NODO provided the only visual information on monthly events that we learned about on the radio or in the newspaper. It was really a brief overview of political activity that extolled the actions of the government. Among the many inaugurations of reservoirs and nuclear powerplants, and scenes of the dictator deep sea fishing, the NODO provided a summary of international news. I remember vividly images of the Korean War, from 1951 to 1953, when I was five to seven years old. They also replayed images of the atomic bombs that fell over Hiroshima and Nagasaki a few years earlier. For some reason, those scenes are burned into my retina, as are other newscasts of the wars in Vietnam (1955-1975) and Cambodia (1967-1975).

Perhaps those searing boyhood memories were what provoked such an intense emotional response, when I visited Hiroshima, Ho Chi Minh, and Phnom Penh, many years later. I'm against war, no matter the cause or reason. I'm opposed to using force, even in self-defense. I believe that wars have never solved any conflict, but they do tend to aggravate them. The great playwright Bertolt Brecht wrote something that rings true for me:

The war that will happen
is not the first.
There were other wars.
At the end of the last
there were victors and victims.

Among the victims,
the simple folk went hungry.
Among the victors,
the simple folk went hungry too.

(Bertolt Brecht)

In 2010, I arrived at Japan on a ship that went around the world for a university Semester at Sea program. From the port of Kobe, Carrie and I took a bullet train to Hiroshima. I love trains and the autumn landscape became more and more charming as we passed tiny immaculate villages laid out in perfect order. It was a pilgrimage to the city punished by the most violent and terrible atomic attack ever suffered. Today it's a monument to peace. We arrived in Hiroshima, a serene and orderly city, like all of Japan. What remains of the bombarded city are two buildings that have been left to stand as monuments to peace so that no one forgets. As someone who carries an American passport, I must accept my part of the blame. Hiroshima leaves an impression. There's no way to justify such an atrocity and tragedy. I'm not sure we've fully grasped the consequences of that atrocious act.

HIROSHIMA, MON AMOUR

How to love you in Hiroshima?
With what rifle, spoon, or chalice?
Which dove to save and for what cause?

Perhaps I saw it in a film, or I dreamed it.
It will not happen during my stay.
I'll pass through leaving a trace of my scent,

without counting the dead or preserving them.
I'll remember the photos and newsreels.
I won't ask questions. Words are not enough.
Neither genuflecting nor beating the chest.

Neither the past nor the dead
return when summer bids farewell
and shadows slip round the sundial.

Picasso's dove died in Hiroshima.
How to make love to you
when desire sleeps
moored to the marble of the memorial?

(From *La vuelta al mundo en 80 poemas/
Around the World in 80 Poems*)

Sitting next to my grandmother in the Montija Theater, the war was a collage of faraway images in black and white. In the museum in Hiroshima, the exhibit descriptions blame the Nipponese generals for the ferocious consequences of the war and its final outcome, and not the United States and its killing machine. I don't know what made me a detractor of all wars and their violence, whether it was my grandmother, or the war my father bore witness to, or my mother's fear of thunder that she mistook for bombardment.

In Kyoto, the experience was quite different. Its gardens are hymns to peace and havens for the spirit. It's not surprising that the primary religions are Shintoism and Buddhism, religions without a repressive god.

38

We arrived at Los Antiguos, a town on the Buenos Aires Lake, which measures 2240 square kilometers, so large it looks like the sea. The lake sits high in the Andes, with one side bordering Argentina and the other neighboring Chile. It was a calm afternoon and after dropping off our luggage at the hotel, we went for a walk beneath the lush canopy of tree-lined sidewalks leading to the still waters of the lake. Right away, we noticed the photograph of a young man's beautiful face plastered on the walls of shops and on trees and light posts. The afternoon turned into evening, and then came a decent meal in one of the local family restaurants. Who knows what we ate. Darkness turned to light, and night to morning, but the photograph remained in the same places as a reminder or warning of something. It was hard to know what because there was no name, date, or dedication. Simply the face of a young man whose eyes were fixed on ours.

We packed our things and put them in our little red car and got ready to leave, but first we stopped at a bakery to buy provisions for the next leg of our journey. Mempo and I had been traveling for more than four weeks since leaving Resistencia, following the river south to Buenos Aires, then continuing along the coast toward Mar del Plata, Puerto Madryn, Península Valdés, Rawson, all the way to Río Gallegos and El Calafate. From there, we'd ascended the mythical Route 40, which in the year 2000 wasn't paved, meaning we had to travel over a dusty road of dirt and gravel. As we were paying, we asked the owner of the bakery about the photo. Mempo told her he was interested because he was a journalist and was writing pieces for newspapers in the capital. This sparked her interest, and after leading us into the back of the shop, she told us a sad and macabre tale that reflects the impunity with which legal matters are handled in many small towns. It's one of those stories that, when told in a soft voice in a bakery of a forsaken town in Patagonia, sounds like something straight out of a novel. But it wasn't fiction.

What she told us was that about a year ago, the young kid in the photo had gone out with friends to celebrate reaching the legal age of eighteen. He came upon a group of local guys, well-known in the town, including plain-clothes officers, the mayor, and a bunch of friends who'd been drinking and promised to make a real man out of him. Intimidated, the young boy followed them. They took him to an empty house, stripped him, covered his body with la-tex paint, tied a rope around his penis, and paraded him through the streets of the town while laughing and making crude jokes. After what seemed an eternal torture, the boy began to scream that his skin was burning from the paint, so they decided to take him back to the house. One of the jokers stuck him in the bathroom to wipe off the paint with gasoline. The cigarette hanging from the mouth of the sup-posed savior sparked the flames that engulfed the body of the boy who, helpless, ran out of the house and rolled on the grass trying to extinguish the inferno consuming him. The protagonists scattered quickly, while one of the boy's friends called his mother who took charge of her son's charred body. Still hopeful, she took him to the closest city, and on the way, the boy recounted the ordeal to his mother. Finally, he was transferred to a hospital in Buenos Aires that specialized in burns. There was no hope. He took his final breath soon after arriving. The mother returned to Los Antiguos to bury her son and was shocked to hear that nothing had happened in the town that night, and no one remembered a thing. Her son's story was fiction, or "fake news," that current expression made popular by the President of the United States. Appealing for justice was a useless act on her part. Her testimony was dismissed because she was the mother of the victim. The friend's eyewitness account as well because he was a minor. The courts put a lid on the case.

The baker asked us to visit the mother before we left town, and we did. The distressed mother filled in the holes of the story the bakery owner had told us. Mempo wrote an article about the episode and sent it to newspapers in Buenos Aires, but not one published it. We left the town while the eyes from all the photographs on the walls and trees watched us depart. Feelings of anguish and impotence accompanied us the following days, and still do now as I write this. His story appears in the book that Mempo published about our journey, *Final de novela en Patagonia* (*End of a Novel in Patagonia*), recipient of the Premio Grandes Viajeros (Great Traveler's Prize) in 2000.

39

We spend our lives in front of the mirror. We look at ourselves in the morning when we wake up and wash our face and wipe the sleep from our eyes. Whenever we go to the bathroom, we check out our hair and our same old face. We give one more look at our attire before heading out the door and take another look at night while we brush our teeth in our pajamas. We even glance at ourselves in the shop windows we pass on the sidewalk, and constantly turn to the mirror to check our emotional state and smile at what we see or dislike. For some, it's an occupation, for others a sport or pastime. This provocative face-off with the mirror always presents a challenge of sorts. Over time we create a mask we offer others. In my case, I started growing a beard and let it take over my face, lending me a mature intellectual air. It was black, almost blue, rugged, flamboyant, like that of a prophet, I'd venture to say. I wore it for more than twenty-five years, until I needed a jaw operation and shaved it off, keeping a thick moustache, sort of like Omar Shariff with a Don Juan flair, a resemblance I've never rejected or desired. My father wore his hair like Rudolph Valentino, plastered down, like a tango singer's. He never wore a moustache, that thin moustache popular among Franco's followers after the war. My father was a bit of a dandy. You can see that in the few photos we have of him in the family album that's been handed down as one relative after another passed away.

Until her death, my mother dyed her hair chestnut brown. In her old age, she had a beautiful silvery white mane that she wanted to color out of vanity. For a while, with my beard, black beret, and a pipe without tobacco, I looked like Che Guevara, an idol for so many. At one point, I shaved off my moustache and beard giving my chin a more youthful appearance, although at that stage of the game, bags had appeared under my eyes and there was nothing young about me.

The mirror kept looking at me and I gazed back at it. Who's fooling whom? Not long ago, I grew a beautiful white beard and let my hair grow long. That's when the mirror announced the arrival of old age with no pretense, although when I'm in the gym, surrounded by mirrors, the figure I see, holding a weight in each hand, attempts to reflect an image of inextinguishable vitality. I've added a diamond stud to my left earlobe, and I change glasses now and then to match the image of the one I desire to be, the one I project to the world and those closest to me, even though my true self remains inside me. I worry more about that other self, the one I can't see in the mirror. That image is only reflected in what others perceive, in my actions, my commitments, my loyalty, energy, and accomplishments.

40

I grew up in the home of a religious family, where my mother and father had infused their love and plans for the family with religious values. They attended mass on Sundays and celebrated all religious holidays. They treated Holy Week as if were a funeral for a relative, organized first communion for their children, and observed the many rites of the Christian doctrine. At night, their voices traveled down the hallway as they recited the rosary in unison, while picking up the chaotic mess their four children left behind after hours of free-wheeling play.

Like my siblings, I attended a Catholic school, the first one run by nuns, then another directed by los Hermanos de las Escuelas Cristianas de La Salle, and later an academy managed by Jesuits. Despite that, religion didn't have much of an impact on me personally. I considered its rites and ceremonies cultural practices, for example, the festival of San Isidro, where we'd go to the saint's shrine and drink water from the miraculous fountain, or Midnight Mass on December 24th, when we'd sing Christmas songs. In Spain, Catholicism was more than a religion, it was a culture. And still is today. Yet, when I became a member of the *Hogar del Empleado* organization, I experienced intimate feelings of another nature. The evening meditations around the campfire, surrounded by mountains scented by woods and illuminated by stars, left their mark on me. Nature fused with a universal concept of God the Creator. On several occasions, they encouraged me to conduct spiritual exercises first conceived by Ignacio, the founder of the Jesuit Order. I requested permission from the company where I worked to spend a week in the mountains to carry out those exercises. They granted it and I spent seven days in the Guadarrama mountains, in a house with a garden, reading, meditating, praying, and pondering how to overcome the desires of the flesh, an unfortunate choice of words to refer to sex. This was the part I struggled with the most. Sex has always been problematic in my life. Isn't it for everyone? The idea of renouncing sex for religious reasons seemed horrendous to me and may have changed my destiny. Despite my skepticism, one foggy morning while I gazed at the landscape bathed in nostalgia and dew, I experienced an almost physical awareness of a divine presence. For the first and only time, I believed that God existed because I'd felt his presence. That revelation turned all my thoughts upside down and what had been mere habits became a new way of life. From then on, I started to commit foolish acts based on bizarre theological ideas. During those spiritual exercises, they convinced me of the redeeming impact of sacrificing my body, so I bought a cilice, a kind of instrument of torture or self-torture. You tie it tightly around the thigh and walk while wearing it. As the muscle expands, the barbs of the cilice pierce the skin, resulting in pain. The theological concept, God knows who invented it, was that suffering in the present moment has a retroactive effect that allows our suffering to relieve the affliction felt by Christ on the cross. My mother, as religious as she was, would hide those cilices so I couldn't wear them. I'd buy others. She'd tell me I was crazy and that the practice was unacceptable and excessive. What religion did she practice? Did she think my father could be saved by her vigils, prayers, and sacrifices? When she lay at death's door, what heaven did she think she'd enter? Isn't that the attraction of all religions?

My excessive acts during those years of Christian fervor were many. My hours of prayer and meditation as well. I went to confession every day until a priest took pity on me and told me I didn't have to confess every act of masturbation. That primal faith vanished as quickly as it arrived, without anguish or concern. It happened when I discovered the naked body of a woman. I recall the verses of Blas de Otero: "When I saw you, oh bare and blossoming body, I believed I saw God in the flesh." When I gazed up at the summer sky, I saw just a lofty blue sky with clouds and swallows. Ever since then, organized religions make me cringe with scorn. Granted, I realize this is my personal experience with religion and we should always show respect for religions provided their doctrines don't restrict the freedom of others. That's my way of thinking – absolute freedom to be what we should be. My personal creed. Who taught me that? Did it come from my father's sense of humanity, my mother's silent tolerance, the Jesuit teachers at the academy, the Marxist professors at the university, my friends from all walks of life, my diverse and profusive readings, or from that one inside me, the conscience shaped by good intentions and tenderness. Who knows?

Our Father, I know not if thou art in heaven,
if thy name be hallowed, or where
amongst so many republics, thy kingdom lies.
My will – perhaps that of many –
is to survive on this thirsty
and unjust earth. Our daily bread,
doled out metaphorically, runs scarce.

Who will forgive us our debts?
Perhaps the banks?
As for me, no one owes me a dime.
So, I've done my part there.
Oh, how I'd love to fall into temptation
and let wanton flesh entice me,
till the end of my days,
with no resistance on my part. Amen.

(From *Pureza demolida/
Ravaged Purity*)

41

From the tenth floor of Hofstra University's Axinn Library, you can see the skyscrapers of Manhattan. Off in the distance, they look like abandoned columns of a Greek metropolis, but they have little in common with the somber Parthenon or the impressive architecture of those temples. Yet, temples they are. They adore other gods, facilitate other transactions, and shelter the bustling finance capital of the world. I had my first glimpse of that magical city in 1974. Carrie and I had traveled there from Boston by Greyhound bus, the transportation for many in the U.S. with limited means. It was the initial stage of our romance, and upon arriving to Manhattan, we camped out in the apartment of a friend of hers. Back then, I was the product of Franco's Spain and had been raised and educated under a system of unjust justice. The city made a profound impression on me from the start. The diversity of the neighborhoods, with their restaurants from so many places, formed a kaleidoscope only possible on that island: neon lights, billboards, attractions, thousands of feet walking in different directions without tripping or scuffling, museums, skyscrapers, and a steady stream of vehicles and souls flowing along canyon-like avenues. I looked without seeing. I couldn't take it all in. Something special was brewing in that city I'd barely begun to explore.

My second trip was in 1978, after we'd moved to Virginia. I went there to pick up my mother, who came to visit us when my first son Philip was born. I was so happy to welcome her and see once again the childish expressions on her face. She seemed like a little girl who couldn't suppress her delight and apprehension. We walked through Chinatown and took the metro through endless tunnels as if on a journey to another time. Ever since then, I've been attached, through family ties, to this metropolis that defies description. Two of my children, Philip and Camila, have lived there for a sum of twenty years. Perhaps that's why I've visited the city so often. I took one of my last trips to meet my daughter Marta, who traveled there for a reunion after forty years of estrangement.

More than 330 languages are spoken in New York City, which means that at least somebody can speak one of them. In Manhattan alone there are 24,000 restaurants and 696 hotels, but believe it or not, Manhattan is a small island of only fifteen miles from one end to the other. My memories are sprinkled with moments of delight and threat. The Manhattan I knew or know is not the indefensible city of marginalized neighborhoods entrenched in drugs. The Bronx and Harlem, at the north end of the island, were borders that if crossed led into a human jungle. Taxis refused to go there and anyone with common sense would advise you to stay away. Over the years, the area has become more civilized, and today you can stroll through its serene neighborhoods, if you can call them that.

My son and I decided one day to explore that area, from Battery Park, at the southernmost end, to the Cloisters at its northern point. It was a pilgrimage of sorts to savor its diverse character, step by step. Those who walk can recognize the bricks and cobblestones, appreciate the trees and facades, smell the thyme and fried food, and listen to the breezes and tribal rhythms. Those familiar with this universal city know its neighborhoods represent mini kingdoms: Soho, Little Italy, Chinatown, Wall Street, Time Square, Greenwich Village, Hudson Yards, Central Park, Harlem, and Hamilton Heights, neighborhoods that have forged distinct identities within a limited space. I've made that pilgrimage several times, alone and with Eliseo Valle, my dear friend from Cuenca who's a great talker and all-around good guy.

I love to walk whenever I travel, observing and absorbing my surroundings with no internal restraints. I entitled one of my books of poetry *Ciudades de tiza. Paisajes de papel.* It's a book about cities that's inspired by them. My theory is that cities speak, although in diverse ways and in other codes. The challenge is to decipher them as if they were polygraphs, even though the translation isn't solely oral or written, but visual. The faces, advertisements, facades, and walls tell the tale of a city built by individuals, society, and architects who left their mark. In that volume of poems, I tried to transcribe what the streets and buildings told me in their unique forms and intonations. To my surprise, I discovered a lot in the process. Certain cities don't seem to say much, or at least I couldn't perceive anything. Others were tireless communicators, indomitable chatterboxes. I took special notice of this when I took on the role of scribe for my book *Ciudades de tiza*. New York is one of those cities. It never stops talking or communicating its numerous messages. It opens its doors and seduces us, laughing and singing to the beat of its varied rhythms.

For many years, we held family reunions in New York at Christmastime. The avenues have a magical air about them when snow falls softly from a ceiling of skyscrapers. With their decorated window displays, the grand department stores try to create a special Christmas spirit. Some would call it commercial. Nowadays, Christmas is celebrated around the world as a commercial experience. For decades, I rejected during the holidays what I considered a forced joyfulness that put me in a bad mood. Now I know my attitude originated in the fact that my father died five days before Christmas, casting a shadow of sorrow difficult for me to overcome. My father, who spent so much energy and care setting up the nativity and procuring holiday foods from his hometown for what seemed a bountiful celebration, ruined the party for us. It's taken me years to recapture that happiness. I did so by wrapping myself in the joyful excitement of my children and the neon lights of New York shimmering over the facade of Rockefeller Center. But New York City is much more than all that. Perhaps it's the museum of all museums, the theater of all theaters, the celebration of encounters, the arrival and crossing from one border to another, with nearly each step, in the faces of pedestrians wearing felt caps and wool coats. New York is also the world of all worlds, the place where people converge inevitably at every turn.

Here we are, ladies and gentlemen,
without a doubt. This is
the modern Babel.

Here the wind dons
a turban and in the morning
swirls round the pearl markets.

Korea is here, Bangladesh,
Marco Polo's Venice,

and the most ancient Confucius.
Avenues straight as an arrow
are Olympic tracks
where the most spurious
desires compete
at a democratic pace.

In New York we are all
New Yorkers for an instant
while strolling through Soho,
wandering down Fifth Avenue
enticed by impossible desires,
or feasting on spaghetti
in Little Italy.

We down a universal swig
that vanishes, alas,
once we return home.

But for a few hours, misery
and orchids promenade
hand in hand, or nestle
pensively in the dark
heart of injustice.

Here they celebrate sushi,
hearts of palm, merengue,
opera, the blues,
Puccini or Mozart,
with hot peppers, vodka, or caipirinha,
as if a collage of senses
were all the rage.

Here, you and I, the firefighter,
the nurse, my lover,
her naked inflamed flesh,
desire, the Twin Towers
reduced to debris, the nose
sniffing round the ashes,
and the deep sky
over its vertical stage,
for an instant,
makes each of us citizens,
distinct and unique
inhabitants of this urban universe
that expands with no room to stretch,
bursting the island at the seams.

(From *Ciudades de tiza. Paisajes de papel /
Chalk Cities. Paper Landscapes*)

42

Many homes sheltered me as I grew up, dreamed, and fell in love. They were silent and complicit witnesses to my shenanigans, restlessness, boredom, and labor. I was born on a street in the heart of Madrid, in one of its most traditional neighborhoods, Argüelles. We lived in a basement apartment with windows that looked out on a courtyard with mulberry trees whose berries stained the ground with juice the color of blood in the spring. That's where I spent a happy childhood playing games, some not so innocent that would make today's liberal mothers blush. We spent all day in that yard, regardless of rain or heat. We'd perch in the treetops and spy through windows of the upper floors like voyeurs while smoking anise cigarettes sold at the kiosks where we got candy.

The lifesaver in our house was the *botijo*, a large clay jug that sat on the dining room sideboard. We'd flock to it for fresh water to quench our thirst. There were no soft drinks or sodas of any kind, only water from a *botijo* that my father bought at the annual San Isidro festival by the Manzanares River. We were conceived in that apartment and raised with much love and our share of hard times. We held the wake for my father in that apartment when his time came. Shortly after his death, residents were told the apartments would be sold and were given the option to buy or move. Money was tight, so we had to pack our things without knowing where we'd go. Back then, my mother and her four kids lived in that apartment, along with my maternal grandparents. My grandfather retired with a modest pension, and my grandmother received even less as a housewife. My mother managed the situation with trepidation but without faltering, as women do when faced with a crisis. We ended up in the Usera neighborhood where my Uncle Paco lent us the small apartment he'd acquired for his upcoming retirement. There we set up what you could call a winter camp with a hodgepodge of furniture, mattresses, and rugs, a chaotic battleground that drove us to spend most of our time outside.

A year later, Fabra y Coats, the company I worked for, rented us an apartment in a building of dwellings constructed with the paternalistic attitude of those businesses aligned with fascist nationalism, during Franco's regime. Salaries were meager but modest bonuses were offered to keep protests at bay or create a false sense of social consciousness. The entire brood moved there with all our belongings. Those were the early years of television, which we watched in our neighbors' upstairs apartment. They'd attached a color filter to their set, giving it the feeling of technicolor, which already existed in the United States, birthplace of all technological advances. We were familiar with technicolor from watching Hollywood movies. When I figured out that our low rent apartment was a trap to keep me indentured for the rest of my professional life, I rebelled. I found a better paying job and told my mother we had to leave that apartment. That was like a dagger to her heart. Her son's selfishness was forcing the family clan to pack up once more and move to another place, neither better nor worse, but with less light and the same financial woes, perhaps even more. During the day, two mattresses rested on top of a wardrobe. At night, we'd put them on the floor and that's where my brother José

Luis and I would sleep. When morning came, the mattresses returned to the stratosphere of the wardrobe. The apartment was in Carabanchel, a working-class neighborhood with a bullring from the days when the area was a town on the outskirts of the city. The *botijo* was replaced by an icebox, a small cabinet lined with aluminum. It had a cooling coil at the top and everyday a block of ice would be placed on the coil to keep the inside cold and the water cool. The rest of the food was kept fresh during the winter in a wooden box lined with metallic mesh, which was placed outside the kitchen window. Madrid's cold temperatures preserved the food. Today, as I describe these delirious homespun inventions, I feel as if I grew up in another era.

I left that house after my first marriage, soon after turning twenty-two. We made a lovebird nest in a newly constructed apartment in the Aluche neighborhood and went about decorating it to our tastes. We painted the walls white and red and even papered some of them. It's best not to talk about what happened there or write about it. Let's just say there was a lot of love but also tragedy. For reasons I won't mention, we moved to another apartment in the Batán neighborhood, and from there, a year later, I made plans to start over in Barcelona when our young marriage fell apart due to our mutual immaturity and inability to find a solution to our problems.

Barcelona lit up my life with a stream of light after years of myopia. It's not that I didn't see clearly before, just the opposite, but I felt a renewed sense of hope. I had nowhere to live or rest my bones, but that didn't matter as much as the sensation of freedom. Freedom of all kinds: of religion, entertainment, dreams, nudity on the beaches at dusk, aimless walks along the Ramblas during the evening hours, and the liberty to rant and rage against the dictatorship. I made new friends and felt loved in a place where four of us banded together to meet our basic needs. We changed apartments several times, decorating each one with a Picassoesque-frenzy but with no Picasso. We rescued furniture from the street to fill our empty rooms. An abandoned fruit crate became my nightstand. Brothers in solidarity, we hung all our clothes in the entryway closet, and laughter rang out amid deprivation. Each of us had our own personal wounds and together we nursed and tried to heal them. It was a time when questions weren't asked and a knowing look sufficed. This all happened while we worked, studied at the university, and sought refuge on the beaches of the Costa Brava. It lasted until love returned and each of us left with our partners. I met Carrie and we moved to La Floresta, a vacation town on the other side of Montjic, where we stayed in a tiny house with a garden of rose bushes and hydrangeas. We lived there as a couple, traveled throughout Europe, and made plans for the big leap to America.

Virginia is a garden, a green meadow surrounded by hills and the Appalachian Mountains, which extend for two thousand miles from Vermont to Georgia. We started out in a little prefabricated house in the middle of a farm that once raised rabbits for the university's laboratories. I felt more out of place there than a burro in a garage. I looked to the east where the forest grew, shrouded in mystery. In front of the house was a wooded hill inviting me to climb, something I did every day. We spent the first summer tending a garden on that farm, thirteen miles from Charlottesville. Perhaps it was the most beautiful experience of that menacing summer. I'm not a handy man, in fact, I don't like manual labor. I can change a lightbulb and paint a wall, but not much more. The main problem is I hate to read manuals. Even so, I found something magical and sensual about that garden. To open the earth with a hoe and plant a seed is a mysterious act, seemingly insignificant, but to watch a green sprout rise from the dark earth elicits a special emotion, akin to life's most basic and fundamental truth. We planted everything in that garden with enthusiasm but without an organized plan: tomatoes, potatoes, kale, spinach, lettuce, corn, carrots, cabbage, okra, zucchini, cucumbers, and peppers. Everything grew like crazy. Rows of corn adorned with golden ears grew tall, tomatoes brightened the mornings, onion stalks rose straight and graceful, not to mention the round pumpkins fattened in the red earth, like in a Cinderella story, and nourished by Virginia's frequent rain.

Everything has a downside, and our experience as farmers turned out to be overwhelming. We didn't know what to do with two hundred pounds of potatoes, dozens of ears of corn, basket upon basket of tomatoes that rotted unless we spent grueling hours canning them. We even bought equipment for that. While Virginia's heat and humidity took their toll on us, our first son announced his arrival. We had to decide what to do with our lives. It was an interesting experience that's hard for me to describe. It was exciting but almost did me in. Not because of the physical labor of an amateur farmer, which I enjoyed and learned so much from, but for the solitude I endured.

Once we were accepted as doctoral students at the University of Virginia, we moved to the city and rented a duplex in a neighborhood on the outskirts of town. It was a tiny but charming house with a little yard by a stream. We planted brussel sprouts and spinach. Because we couldn't afford the rent, we shared the place with a young mother who'd just returned from Dharamsala, India. She'd lived there for a few years and had converted to Buddhism and had a son with a monk. The boy was named Jason and was the same age as our Philip. They became friends and played together. They cared for a rabbit we kept in a cage in the yard and showered him with affection. One morning, we found the rabbit dead. Philip cried his little heart out. Jason went inside with his mother and together they did what was necessary to prepare the rabbit for reincarnation. The next day, Jason came to us smiling and told us that the rabbit was now a horse that grazed peacefully nearby. I consider that an efficient way of dealing with adversity, or the tragedies life throws in our path. On the other side of our house were two trailers that housed some old folks, several young men and women, a group of individuals difficult to describe, and a boy with blond hair and big blue eyes. That boy also made friends with Philip and Jason, and together they rode tricycles, dodging hens raised in that trailer camp. The boy's father was in jail for murdering the mother. Someone, maybe the grandparents, took care of him. In their backyard was a chaotic pile of furniture, appliances, bicycles, and cars. Probably the bounty of their robberies. We never knew much about that, nor did we want to. They assured us that because we were neighbors and our son played with their grandson-nephew, nothing would ever happen to us, and our humble possessions would be safe.

It was a difficult but enjoyable time when we had unstable incomes and two sons to feed. We were living in that place when our second son Peter was born. Even with meager salaries, we didn't hesitate to take long trips in a Chevy van we bought from an English couple who was returning to their country. On several occasions we imitated the journeys of Jack Kerouac and traveled across the country visiting beautiful national parks in the west (Monument Valley, the Colorado Canyon, Yosemite, Yellowstone, Arches National Park, Devil's Tower, Badlands National Park, among others), even dipping into the waters of the Pacific in California.

We bought our first house on Calhoun Street in Charlottesville. Up until then, for my first thirty-five years, I lived in rented places. Something special happens when you live in your own house and take care of it as you would your own children. We were living in that house when Camila was born. With her, I took on the full responsibility of fatherhood, with all the stress and ravings of a father struggling to adjust to that role, while juggling romantic fantasies, desires for freedom, and passions for traveling, creativity, and sports. Life isn't easy. It's a continuous apprenticeship that makes us take refuge from the rain even on days when it's not raining.

The final stop has lasted thirty years in a typical Virginian house very near the university campus. Majestic trees surround the house, sheltering it from the heat and cold, while thoughtlessly shedding their fruit, juice, and debris. I'm talking about pollen, nuts, dry leaves in the fall, and every now and then, tired branches. This house is now the center for gatherings of our extended family. The children who grew up in its rooms and garden left one by one after going to college and finding jobs as far away as possible. That's another one of those rites of passage of the American middle-class society. Our children moved to Washington, D.C., and New York. They fell in love and married. Over the passing years, they come back to visit us with their children. The cycle has ended and come full circle.

43

The first school I attended at the age of four was Patrocinio de María de las Hermanas de la Caridad, an institution run by nuns on Madrid's Gaztambide Street. I don't know what they taught us or what we learned. Next to the tiny school was a church that cared for disadvantaged seniors. In the large dining room, which was actually the auditorium or assembly hall, we children ate lunch at noon with the old folks. Images from childhood remain fixed in the mind, images we can't understand to this day. What I remember are old toothless people eating rice pudding, the white substance dribbling from the corners of their lips and grains of rice falling onto the tablecloth. An Italian neorealistic image. Ever since, I've had a phobia about rice pudding, even though I love milk and rice is one of my favorite grains. How cruel we can be as children. The sisters wore black habits at all hours, with rosaries of large beads and scapularies hanging from their necks. They wore a sort of starched white bonnet that looked like a small airplane parked on their heads, ready for takeoff. We sang, that's for certain. In fact, I remember one school festival at which we performed a medley of Basque songs, dressed in white like natives of Pamplona, with red sashes and berets tilted to the side. I remember that outfit because it was captured in a photo, one of the few from my childhood preserved in the family album that has been handed down after the passing of each custodian.

My mother was the first custodian and protected it like a golden treasure. In it are photos of Papá and Mamá strolling down the Gran Vía of Madrid, and others of them at someone's wedding, and at their own, the bride dressed in black. There are photos of baptisms, and some taken in the summer in the mountains outside Madrid, in the towns of Collado Mediano and Cercedilla. When my mother died, the album was passed down to Lourdes, my sister, the guardian of family memories. She knew by heart the dates of all births and weddings. She never forgot a name and preserved in her memory a cherished collection of family stories. She remembered events that happened at home, in the neighborhood, or anecdotes from when we all lived together, maybe because she was the oldest and had lived longer than her brothers. She would've been a great help now as I delve into the past in search of light amid so much darkness. After her death, the family album disappeared like Eva Perón's body, stolen after it was embalmed. After a few years of uncertainty, the album reappeared, dismantled, in the house of my brother-in-law, widower of my sister. Now it's safeguarded by my brother Mariano, second in line. I must go to his house and capture on my iPhone those moments of so many years of family life. I don't know why, perhaps in the future this will be of interest to my children, when their own have grown up and it's time for them to transmit the chronicle. It's much easier today because everything is recorded and saved forever in a cloud, that strange, incomprehensible, mythical place where supposedly everything we write, record, or photograph is stored. After the death of her father, my wife spent months digitalizing thousands of photos from more than one hundred albums, which will eventually go up to the sky, to that cybernetic cloud whose future is as confusing as my understanding of the phenomenon.

After seven decades, I still can't eat rice pudding and the ominous image of those toothless old people rises to the surface and ruins any attempt I make. I believe growing old is cruel. We no longer have grace, agility, or energy. We become clumsy in our movements and fumble to rationalize and remember. Everything becomes coated with forgetfulness and at the end all that's left is pity. The movie *The Curious Case of Benjamin Button*, with Brad Pitt, tells the story of a boy who's born an old man, and as time passes, he returns to middle age, youth, and childhood, and finally to the moment of death before conception. An interesting alternative.

From that school, with its flying nuns, milky dining hall, and basic grammar lessons, what I don't forget is the ringing of the final bell in the afternoon when we boys would stand on the curb of the sidewalk and compete to see who could make a fine stream of urine reach the sidewalk on the other side of the street. Did we ever reach it? Were our tiny penises the ridiculous image of our desire to conquer what lay before us? Did no one ever say a thing to us while the nuns hid in the darkness of the cloister?

44

I visited India on a trip I took later in life. Few trips have impressed me as much as that one. India is another world, an incomprehensible otherness far-removed from my Argüelles neighborhood with its shops and squid sandwiches. It has nothing to do with the tango or country music, hamburgers, or the dead silence of downtown US cities that took me so long to get used to. In other words, India is so far removed from the West, and proud of that distance. Upon arrival to the port of Chennai (previously Madras), the first and strongest impression is the odor of multitudes. Vehicles of all kinds flow like rivers, chaotic streams of people cross paths erratically with no apparent course or direction, getting in each other's way, passing and looking at each other, engaging or disregarding one another. Their presence represents a fraction of the billion inhabitants of that country.

In a school for the arts, a traveling theater troupe performed several scenes from the *Mahabharata*. The complete version takes eight hours to stage. The *Mahabharata* is the national epic poem whose origins date back to 400 B.C., and a longer version to 400 A.D. Before the play begins, the actors spend hours on make-up, a ceremonious act as ritualistic as the performance itself. For the most part, I don't stand on ceremony, but I find something special about rituals. Over the years, the West stripped away ceremonies and rituals, leaving itself somewhat bare, especially after certain revolutions (bourgeois, anti-clerical, and hippie), and the vanguardist and postmodern movements. What I liked most about the years I attended church and Catholic school were the ceremonies and musical rituals of the Gregorian mass. If there truly is a God, He must be present in the sublime virtue of certain rituals. It seems that in India, life itself, even its most insignificant moments, are immersed in ritual. Problems may arise when their meanings are misunderstood.

New Delhi is an enormous metropolis with an elegant downtown and aspires to become the cultural capital of India, a country that continues to expand in the 21st century. Although it has a spectacular imperial center, 70% of its population lives in poverty. Beggars plague the efforts of city planners. From Delhi we traveled by train to Agra, the city dominated by the Mughal empire for centuries. The Mughals left their mark on the many forts, palaces, and tombs they erected, the most famous being the Taj Mahal, overlooking the shores of the Yamuna River with its unmatched serenity. But the highlight of our trip was the visit to Varanasi, which truly blew our minds. It's a city founded on several thousand years of religious rituals that honor the pantheon of Hindu gods. It's estimated some three hundred thousand representations of divinities comprise the amazing tribute to the gods revered and adored by Hindus. The city seems to revolve around rituals of incantations along the sacred Ganges River, where ceremonies and cremations are held daily. One day, we attended a grand religious celebration at sunset, and observed in the early morning, from a boat in the river, thousands of the faithful perform their oblations, entering the river and bathing and drinking its sacred, albeit extremely contaminated waters. We also witnessed cremations and watched them cast ashes that were carried by the currents, destined for the sewers, along with everything else, excrements of cows and water buffalo that roam streets, court-yards, and markets, as if in a no man's land.

To reach the temples of Varanasi, you must venture without hesitation onto avenues teeming with animals and pedestrians, cyclists, and passengers on rickshaws, the most popular form of transportation. There are automobiles, relatively few, circulating wildly as if on a racetrack, their drivers oblivious to all laws or rules. This doesn't seem to matter to anyone, nor does anyone seem to care what their neighbors do, no matter how outlandish the behavior. The streets are full of the faithful, pilgrims, holy men, priests, the disabled, snake charmers, vendors of all kinds, tourists, and beggars, especially beggars. The atmosphere is asphyxiating and magical, unreal, and baffling. I felt as if I were suffering from indigestion of sensations and emotions. I couldn't make sense of it all and so I wrote a poem to express in some way my inability to comprehend what I'd seen. At night, I reread and pondered, or ruminated over what I'd written. One of my colleagues, who'd lived in India, told me that it took him years to digest that stew with such a mishmash of ingredients. I thought that out of respect, I should return to India someday.

A babbling stream of steps
winds its way north,
over paths of trampled dust and purity.
Heading south, to a distant repose,
other feet trudge along,
in an endless pursuit of dreams,
without cursing or uttering a sound,
meditating, selling saris,
breathing summer in,

sleeping by fields of rice
and offering gifts
to the god of fire, to the creator,
the one who gave birth to an elephant
and fasted a thousand days, to the ancient one,
who rose from the sea
and turned into stone,
and to the other one, and the one from far beyond.

This is India, brother,
with no course or rules,
neither good nor evil, male nor female,
with a thousand deities,
music and silence,
in a constant ritual.

(From La vuelta al mundo en 80 poemas/
Around the World in 80 Poems)

45

My mother fell in love again. It was a platonic love. She was a woman of few words but spared none to express her deep admiration for Enrique Tierno Galván, the mayor of Madrid from 1979 to 1986. His image was that of a wise old intellectual who dressed conservatively. He'd been a university professor but had no political experience. He conducted himself as a moderate revolutionary and knew how to inspire citizens of Madrid of all ages. He made them feel proud of their city, a metropolis that had suffered from the trauma of being the capital and hadn't always received the attention it deserved. He did this through his actions and public announcements, which he composed in an 18th century style of Spanish: "At the risk of contradicting what the philosopher says in his second book of *Ethics*, we must discard the outdated notion that a woman is a lesser form of a man. This opinion may be controversial, but speaking directly and frankly, long years of experience substantiate that women are as worthy as men when it comes to the faculties of intelligence. Women are also quite capable solving problems that require strength and physical dexterity, not to mention their vivacious imagination and natural aversion to melancholy, all of which make them happy and always willing to lift the spirits of others" (Tierno Galván, February 9, 1983). Tierno Galván injected the city with a positive energy of renewal and the people of Madrid adored him. Since 1984, he was a professor of political law, and during the transition after Franco's death, he founded a political party called the PSP, the Popular Socialist Party. He ran for election in 1977 under that party. His message didn't catch on and he opted for city administration. He wanted to make the city livable, and, to that end, he protected its historical patrimony and promised to create one park a year, which he did. Death surprised him in 1986, amid a whirlwind of new projects. His funeral attracted one of the largest crowds the city had ever seen. My mother cried for him. She felt a certain affinity to that old politician who was born a year before her: Tierno Galvan in 1918 and she in 1919. On the dresser in her bedroom, she kept a photo of the man who'd been one of the most charismatic political figures of that time.

46

Franco was defeated by an enemy he hadn't counted on, the university. Well into the sixties, a university education was reserved for children of the privileged upper class; however, the Spanish university system followed the Napoleonic model, in other words, attending university was a civic right. Spain adhered to that model and classes began to fill up with young students from middle class families who found within the halls of the university a way to escape a life of mediocrity and aspire to a better future. In fact, under Franco, a university education was free and open to all, with two exceptions, the Universidad de Deusto, governed by the Jesuits, and the Universidad de Navarra, overseen by Opus Dei. The rest were public. Christian authoritarianism combined with the ideology of the Spanish Falange promoted this kind of social policies and a university education became more accessible to the masses. Censorship of what was taught in the classroom was much more complicated than censoring newspapers, cinema, theater, and what was said in the streets. I completed my first year of studies at the Universidad Complutense de Madrid, followed by five more at the Universidad Central de Barcelona. Restrictions in Madrid were stricter than in Barcelona, perhaps because the government, embassies and delegations operated from Madrid, or because the main campus of the university was a mere seven miles from El Pardo where the dictator resided. To enter the buildings of the campus, you had to show a university ID, especially during days of unrest, which were frequent. Between strikes, manifestations, protests, and my own justified or unjustified absences, the days I attended class were few and far between. My initial university experience was quite the deception. I didn't attend a single class in the School of Journalism to which I'd been admitted.

Censorship was more complaisant in Barcelona. Franco had always tried not to alienate the Catalonians whose upper class had helped him win the war. From the start, I was surprised by the level of confrontation present within the confines of the university: manifestations, constant protests over the curriculum, strikes, and boycotts of classes taught by professors with dubious political ideologies. If these took place on campus, there were no major repercussions and the forces that maintained public order didn't intervene. It would've been impossible to do so for every provocation. What the dictatorship feared, above all else, were protests and turmoil in the streets that could disrupt the city's tranquil daily life and harm the image of order and peace that the regime wished to project to the world. Official policy maintained that Spain was governed by a structured democracy, given there was a representative parliament called Las Cortes. Even though universal suffrage was not in place, members of parliament served the institutions of the family, trade unions, and the municipality. In other words, parliament functioned as a democracy governed by the laws of the state and not the will of the dictator.

Although my university studies took place under a dictatorship, or *dictadura*, it was more like a dictatorship lite. Generalísmo Franco was growing old and was more interested in fishing and hunting, his two great passions, than running the government. He began to leave matters in the hands of high-ranking ministers, especially Admiral Carrero Blanco whom he named vice-president. The lack of control over universities precipitated the urgent call for change and democracy. The thousands of students who graduated with degrees in technology, humanities, and social sciences formed a core of opposition that transformed Spain from within. When the dictator died in his hospital bed, completely incubated and half-frozen to stop the hemorrhaging of internal organs, the Spanish society had already stopped bleeding and was ready for the next step to normalize public life. That process, known as the Transition, set the stage for the brightest and most resounding moments of Spain's dismal contemporary history.

My mother lived those years through her children. My brother Mariano was the first member of the Operé family to graduate with a university degree. My brother José Luis and I followed him. On the maternal Santillana side of the family, my two cousins Luis and Jaime received degrees in engineering. The next generation, my children and those of my siblings and cousins, also graduated from public universities. This is indeed a leap from the generation of my parents who, between war and poverty, had no choice but to educate themselves on their own. Today the excess of Spaniards with university degrees has created a class of unemployed highly educated citizens who out of desperation search for jobs in other countries of the European Union. Many young, trained professionals have gone to France, Germany, and England, after embracing the ideals of their parents and grandparents who believed that education was a lifesaver. I read this headline in a Spanish newspaper: "More than one million Spaniards with university degrees are at risk of poverty" (October 17, 2018).

47

While pursuing the doctorate in the United States, I had to juggle my studies with work. In the spring of 1980, I spent time in the Washington D.C. area so I could have direct access to the Library of Congress, where I conducted the initial research for my doctoral thesis. The internet didn't exist back then, so you had to use library file cards to search for books and other bibliographic sources. I looked for a job and found a teaching position in a private school in Chevy Chase, a residential area in Maryland close to the capital. My experience as a Spanish teacher for children was an absolute failure, which made me doubt my abilities. Classes ended at three o'clock, at which time I headed for the Library of Congress where I spent long hours until the building closed. I love libraries. Peace and tranquility abide within, enlightened by pages of books and their hidden secrets, and shelves holding collections of documents that contain the knowledge of humanity. It all began with Alexander the Great, who after destroying the Middle East and conquering its villages and people in an unimaginable campaign, fulfilled his incredible dream to build a library that would hold all the books that existed at that time. That was the first great Library of Alexandria. Upon his death, one of his generals, Ptolemy, continued the construction, the first of its kind in the West, although it was a Greek project carried out in Egyptian territory. Alexandria became the center of a civilization that aspired to transcend borders.

Until the 18th century, when the first modern-time libraries were erected, books rested on the shelves of monasteries,
and monks devoted themselves to the work of transcribing
their content into manuscripts so that nothing would ever be
lost. The library of the University of Oxford opened its doors
in 1602. Today it holds 13 million documents. The Library of
Congress was created to serve the needs of the legislative body.
In 1800, John Adams, the second president, approved the act
to create the library and provided it with the first 5000 books.
The collection grew when Thomas Jefferson, the third president, sold 6,487 perfectly catalogued volumes from his personal library in Monticello to support this marvelous library.
Today it has 170 million holdings that include 39 million
printed books in 470 languages, and 73 million manuscripts.
The main reading hall is a gem of modernist architecture. I
spent four months conducting research and reading in that
silent, majestic, and enigmatic space. Its vaulted ceiling, columns, mosaic tiles, and statues created a welcoming refuge
for me as I struggled to overcome sensations of loneliness at a
time when I felt lost because of my inability to speak English
well and the estrangement from my own language.

That sensation was not new to me. I felt the same way in
the National Library of Madrid, when I began my university
studies, and later in the Central Library of the Universidad
de Barcelona, where I spent hours, days, months, and years.
The Alderman Library at the University of Virginia is familiar with my visits and vigils and is aware of my concerns
and doubts. That space has born witness to forty years of my
scholarly labor. During each of my many visits to New York
City, I've always visited the Stephen A. Schwarzman Building of the New York Public Library on 5th Avenue, by Bryant
Park. Other libraries know my preoccupations: the Archivo

General de Indias in Sevilla and the Archivo General de la Nación in Buenos Aires, to mention two of the many libraries where I've spent long periods of time.

The Library of Congress in D.C. is located at the back of the Congress building. The library was erected to serve the needs of senators and representatives. While Alexander the Great invaded, conquered, leveled lands, and enslaved and displaced entire communities, he pursued his universal dream to compile all human knowledge into a gigantic library, one never before seen.

Those first years in Washington spent in the main reading hall of the Library of Congress, spellbound and drowsy, coincided with the presidency of Jimmy Carter, a kind-hearted president – I'm not sure if that's an appropriate term for a president – whose policies suggested that the United States could no longer continue to be the watchdog for international politics, something that didn't go over well with the majority of voters. In the presidential elections of 1980, Carter was soundly defeated by Ronald Reagan, a populist politician who managed the media well, and invited the country to join him in fighting the Empire of Evil, an expression he coined that struck a chord with the nation. Months prior to the elections that year, a mob of fanatics had attacked the North American embassy in Tehran and taken all the officers hostage. It lasted 444 days and initiated a series of Islamic revolutionary movements and a wave of Republican conservativism that named Reagan its champion. The new platforms were based on the creed of individualism and neoliberal economic strategies that advocated cuts in taxes and social programs and gave free reign to corporate industries. Reagan won the elections with 58% of the votes, which allowed him to govern with few obstacles, bolstered by his charismatic personality and the populist message of a powerful and expansive America. A plan was devised in the wings to increase the powers of the presidency in the face of parliamentary safeguards. Under Reagan, the huge multinational corporations and extremely wealthy found a defender who allowed them to think that the end was in sight for the social policies of Franklin D. Roosevelt's New Deal, which had been reinforced by Lyndon B. Johnson's programs for the Great Society and Civil Rights.

George H. Bush succeeded Reagan, followed by his son George W. Bush. The second Bush was more uninformed and relatively easy to manipulate. Dick Cheney, his vice president, was his mentor and behind the efforts to strengthen the prerogatives of the presidency. He pushed the bombing and invasion of Baghdad, based on the false premise that Hussein possessed and would use weapons of mass destruction. It's estimated that more than 400,000 victims perished in that concocted war, along with the devastation of the city's entire infrastructure. The war cost the North American coffers two trillion dollars.

Donald Trump is a consequence of the strategic plan orchestrated before Reagan was elected. But he's also an abomination. His fundamental message to "Make America Great Again," is a hollow slogan. He harkens back to an America that existed at the end of the Second World War, when American imperialism took over international markets and began a race for the accumulation of grotesque amounts of wealth, the expansion of multinational corporations, unrestrained consumerism, and the unchecked usage of natural resources with total disregard to the environment.

It's an abomination that Trump has sidestepped the conservative plans conceived by the so-called Think Tanks.

Trump is an institution of his own, whose decisions depend on his state of mind or gut reaction. Trumpism is Trump, and once that character disappears, what will happen next is a mystery. Will the Republicans return to their traditional conservative thinking or will the party break into factions? The most harmful aspect of his administration is the racial policies he's promoted, supported by white supremacists whose numbers increased during his presidency. This is the sector of the country that's always existed and fears that the myth of the "melting pot" will become reality. In 2014, 62.6% of the population was considered white. By 2050, that figure will decrease to 43.6%, a demographic fact that terrifies many.

I don't believe that Trump has ever set foot in the Library of Congress or the Public Library of New York, the city in which he has resided most of his adult life. As Trump would put it, only losers visit the library. Winners erect skyscrapers with luxury apartments whose primary buyers are members of the Russian mafia or that of other nations, and possibly members of the Mexican or Colombian cartel who lay waste to this country with crime and narcotics. Despite all that and the dominance of the internet, libraries continue to fulfill their mission, slowly, quietly, without fanfare or slogans. Within their walls, books converse with books, exchanging ideas and rallying around the desire of the people to rise above the turmoil so that we don't forget who we were or what we wish to be.

48

Yesterday morning, when I got to the gym, I ran into a woman I've seen many times there. She's in her sixties or appears to be. Her face shows signs of age and chronic pain. I greet her, but she doesn't respond, and I've never seen her laugh. She has a pronounced hump or deformation of her spine that forces her to walk doubled over. Despite that, in the gym she rides the bicycle, walks on the treadmill, and I've also seen her swim in the Olympic-size pool. I practice these same exercises. Is it a way to keep the myth of eternal youth alive? Should we accept the irrevocable notion of steady decline and death? What straw are we trying to grasp? I believe exercise is good for me. Any pessimistic or nostalgic feeling vanishes after two hours riding the bike on the roads surrounding my city, hiking for a day in the mountains, or playing a game of tennis. Something tells me I should hold on to the notion that physical discipline helps keep my body in tip-top shape. Wishful thinking. Is this a valid proposition or am I just fooling myself, as I often do?

Before, and when I say before, that vague timeframe, I'm referring to the generation of my parents or grandparents. Back then, marriage was the dividing line between youth and adulthood. Couples married and the men became sedentary, unless their jobs demanded physical labor. You never saw men, much less women, exercising outside. Sports were for the young and were replaced by the responsibilities of marriage. It's true that people weren't overweight, not because they exercised, but because cars were scarce, they walked a lot, and their diet consisted of vegetables, greens, fruits, eggs, and fish, the so-called Mediterranean diet. I have no memory of my father exercising in shorts. He'd go along with us on Sunday outings to the park and watch us run around, with a doting smile on his lips as he sat down to read the paper.

One of the monumental projects of the Franco regime was the construction of the Parque Deportivo Sindical off the highway leading to El Pardo. This sports complex designed for the masses was built for workers who could show a labor union ID. It included a variety of exercise facilities, but the crown jewel was a pool of grandiose dimensions: 23,812 square feet. It was inaugurated in 1955 so that working-class citizens of Madrid could have access to a place where they could relax and practice sports. In those days, no one had private pools, and there were only a handful of public pools, all very expensive. And so, on numerous occasions, I'd catch a bus that left from the Moncloa plaza to the pool. We'd spend the day there and pack all kinds of food: the typical Spanish tortilla, sandwiches, fruit, and water. My memory often fails me. Perhaps it was a novel and idyllic place. But I don't think so. Considering the size of the venues, it was the perfect place for spreading germs and illnesses. Some Sundays about 40,000 people crammed into that sports center, and about half that number could be in the water at the same time. They'd rinsed off the sweat from the trip, and anyone could and did relieve themselves in the water. It was hard to get to the edge to dive in. I found old photos of the place on the internet, and with all the people crammed in, it looks more like a refugee camp than a recreation center. The pool at the Parque Sindical represented the Franco regime's attempt to democratize its paternalistic culture for the benefit of the working-class masses. Water and a swimming pool for all. We give thanks to our father the Great Leader, was the message. With no access to other such public facilities, this one fulfilled the mission. I went there often with my siblings and cousins, or with friends from work. There were lines to get in, lines to change clothes in the locker rooms, and even more lines to dip your nose in the water.

One time, we convinced our mother to go with us, despite her reluctance. She went but didn't change clothes. She was dressed in mourning and sat in a chair under a tree. From that vantage point, she watched us go in and out, laughing and playing, while she cried. My mother cried for years, day and night, on workdays or holidays. She cried on birthdays and at night when she'd peek into our rooms to see if we were asleep. That constant lament made me so anxious my reaction was to escape and get away from her. I was incapable of showing empathy or sharing her feelings. That sorry state of mourning lasted many long years. For her, everything was related to her dearly departed husband and father of her children. When she was much older, she began to come out of that state of painful rapture and went along on trips without suffering from the same sadness and nostalgia. She'd always say, "oh, if only your father could see you." When I was appointed a professor at the University of Virginia in the 1980s, she came to visit me, and I invited her to sit in on one of my classes. While I addressed the group of students with all the energy and enthusiasm I could muster, she sat in the front row, wiping her tears away. Inside I knew she was repeating, "oh, if only your father could see you." Later in life, she learned to enjoy the present moment, especially when she'd go somewhere and discover simple and unexpected things that would amuse her while she observed them without a plan or objective. Of course, her pleasure was never complete unless she was surrounded by her children, grandchildren, or sister. The husband of her sister, my Aunt Pura, lived longer than hers. When both sisters were finally widowed, they became inseparable, walking, always talking, and having a good laugh together. My mother never exercised, but she was strong and had incredible resilience, her soul did as well, never faltering amidst the most difficult circumstances. When she was on her deathbed, she remembered that she was going to take a trip to finally see Mariano, her husband who passed away thirty-eight years earlier.

49

I don't recall what music we listened to in my house when I was a kid. We never had a record player and back then no other devices played music. The radio was our only connection to the outside world. Neither of my parents had a musical background or played an instrument. If I try hard to remember, I can see them dancing at village festivals. I'm not certain. Children feel uncomfortable watching their parents being intimate. The music transmitted on the radio was basically Spanish music with a flamenco flair, that is, variations of classic flamenco interpreted by popular artists such as Antonio Molina, Juanita Reina, Lola Flores, and Carmen Sevilla, along with a long list of national folklore singers. Mexican music had hit the airways and you could hear rancheras and corridos, ballads inspired by singers such as Jorge Negrete and José Alfredo Jiménez, who had gained international popularity and even appeared in movies. You could hear tango as well, but nothing compared to the bolero, the most internationally acclaimed type of Latin American music popularized in Cuba, Puerto Rico, and Mexico. Its lyrics spoke the language of love. Like the tango, the bolero is danced in close contact, a form of penetration that begins with a look and lingers over the words of the song. It was a liberating musical movement that appeared at the beginning of the 20th century when erotic innuendos sparked desire for romantic adventure. Everything about the bolero revolves around love, love that bids farewell, that ends, that complains, that can't be forgotten. Thanks to the bolero, popular dance music emerged and spread as form of protest against oppression. People all over the Hispanic world listened and danced to boleros, hummed their melodies, and memorized their lyrics. The compositions and interpretations of Agustín Lara, Antonio Machín, and Los Panchos defined a generation and continue to be popular to this day. Through the open window of the kitchen that looked out on the inner courtyard, my mother listened to a neighbor's radio playing boleros sung by Nat King Cole, whose velvety voice transmitted his own rendition of "Ansiedad," "Bésame, bésame mucho," and "Aquellos ojos verdes." Even now I can still hear in my mind those melodies and how he interpreted the lyrics with a pronounced but seductive gringo accent.

As for the impact of music on my education, it always held a special place in my youth. When I was twelve years old, a classmate and I formed a duet and sang, accompanied by guitars, some of the most popular boleros of the day: "Quiéreme mucho," "Quizás, quizás," "Solamente una vez," "Muñequita linda," "Piensa en mí," and others.

BOLERO

That woman who never loved me
nor stole one of my ribs, offered
her hip on which to swing or rest my hand.
She placed hers on my shoulders,
a gift to the Oracle of Dance while
a hint of her exquisite nudity stirred
beneath the folds of her ballroom skirt.
My hand slid down

her silky dress,
perhaps sensing a burning lust.

That woman teeming with sighs
danced a bolero in my arms,
entwining hers in mine.
My heart, beating to the rhythm,
swirled as it kept pace with steps
gliding toward the desire
of an endless night.
Her legs between mine,
like a drifting sentinel,
willing to embrace the bolero,
belly to belly,
breasts demolishing sorrow,
nostalgic lips whispering
"solamente una vez amé en la vida."

But that was another night and once again
desire dances along the celestial curve
of hips, bodies
entangled in the milky clasp
of thighs, until nearly
the break of dawn when we surrender
to the last beat of the trigger.

(From *Liturgia del atardecer/*
Twilight Liturgy)

They taught music and drawing at the La Salle school I attended. I give credit to my teachers. I had voice lessons in
the choir, directed by Brother Máximo, who was so small

we nicknamed him Hermano Mínimo, Brother Minimum. The repetition of scales helped my strong and vibrant voice, like that of my father, adapt to the melody. We rehearsed the Gregorian mass, which I loved, and other refrains from the sacred liturgy. During the holidays, we sang traditional Christmas songs and others in Latin. And for Saturday mass at the local parish church, we'd sing "Salve Madre." I liked singing in the choir. For me, it represents the miracle that occurs when a collective force becomes energy in unison, blending multiple voices into one. I think when I retire I'll try to learn to read music and join a choir. Even though they gave us voice lessons, they didn't teach us to read music. A shame, but it's never too late. On school field trips, and later during my years of hiking in the mountains, we'd spend most of our time singing. Do they still do that? Or were those innocent times when we all tried to get along? I don't know, but I can say we sang all the time and danced at all the parties.

During my university studies in Barcelona, I discovered many musical talents. Those that impressed me the most were Bob Dylan, Aretha Franklin, Leonard Cohen, and Nina Simone, also the rock and roll of Creedence Clearwater Revival, and jazz. I attended jazz festivals often at the Palau de la Música, that marvelous Modernist building that delights both the senses of sight and hearing. Back then I thought I should learn to play a musical instrument and I opted for the guitar so I could accompany myself while singing. I loved the blues, and my main objective was to play the blues with those provocative rhythms of fingers sliding over guitar strings. I took some classes with Steve, a great North American guitarist, trained in classical guitar, who was married to a Catalonian woman and lived in my neighborhood.

I learned the basics, and at least was able to play songs with simple chords but not much more. I don't have the talent, or I didn't dedicate enough time to it. Much to my surprise, when I moved to the United States, and while I was learning English and tending the garden we'd planted at our little house in North Garden, I offered my services, with my usual chutzpah, as an "entertainer" at bars and restaurants. They gave me a trial run and to my amazement, I was hired at several places: a Mexican restaurant, and a Japanese one, and at several Holiday Inns, where on a 65-foot-high pole by the highway they posted a sign that advertised: "Tonight Featuring Fernando Opere." I still can't believe that. It was a frightening experience. I hadn't rehearsed more than twenty songs and I'd repeat them over and over for four hours, with different intonations and rhythms. They were four endless hours. No one cared about my songs, and no one stopped to listen. I grew tired of my repertoire and hated the melodies I repeated ad nauseum. A hotel lobby is a place where sales and businesspeople pass through without stopping. My guitar and I, perched in a corner of the lobby, seemed an extravagant oddity. They also hired me at a golf club. There they had me meander from table to table displaying my charm and offering my romantic renditions. After a while, I asked myself, who am I fooling? Were our financial needs so dire that I had to subject myself to that farce?

I've sung at many of my friends' weddings and parties. At the university, I organized a musical group with talented students. There were two classically trained guitarists and some of the students had good voices. We put together a repertoire composed of traditional Spanish romances, ballads, and a rich variety of Latin American music. We made the rounds of universities and gave recitals. We even recorded a tape that I must have in some drawer, one of those drawers where we stash things until the day we throw everything away, just when it's needed. There was something special about that experience. My guitar sits in the attic of my house collecting dust. It's waiting for me, and I know I'll return to her like an old love.

My father sang the *jota* every now and then. So did my cousin Charo. It was a way to reclaim their Aragonese roots. I must say that the *jotas* move me. When I listen to them something stirs inside me. During my summer vacations in Benasque, a beautiful town in the Pyrenees province of Huesca, I've heard folkloric groups sing *jotas* at festivals honoring a patron saint, in a traditional and commanding manner. My daughter Camila, who received a musical education in high school and private classes, has a beautiful voice, well-modulated and trained. She sang in an a cappella group in high school and during four years at the university. I'm the father now and enjoy listening to her sing. She works in Manhattan for a music management company. She's my musical advisor and recommends and sends me the latest recordings that might interest me. She knows my tastes, which run the gamut, from Mozart, sacred music, folk music of all kinds, jazz (of which I have a fine collection), and in more recent years, acoustic music, and bluegrass.

50

I've been trying to recollect the years I spent in the army so that I can write about them in this chronicle. They were twenty long months at an age when each day was an opportunity for growth, a setback, or a loss of twenty-four hours. You'd think I could conjure up a slew of stories to tell, but my memory is a barren wasteland when it comes to that time. Antonio Muñoz Molina was able to capture those tragicomic experiences in one of his novels, *Ardor guerrero* (*The Ardor of Warriors*), published in 1995. But I don't know what to write. Was nothing etched in my mind? Didn't a single anecdote from those twenty months in Franco's army leave a mark? My foggy memory does recall that I wasted three months in the town of Móstoles, where the basic training barracks were located. Nationalistic historiography, which is so obsessed with putting patriotic heroes on a pedestal, celebrates two mayors of Móstoles, Andrés Torrejón and Simón Hernández, for signing the Proclamation of Independence against the French invasion of May 2, 1808. It's true the uprising against General Junot lit the spark that ignited a sense of Spanish nationalism, which was in its early stages because of the country's lack of linguistic and cultural integrity and the complex nature of its geography, among other factors. Only the king and the influence of the Catholic Church made up for that lack of coherence and struggled to unite such a diverse kingdom. Even today, we suffer from the negligence that has resulted in exacerbating separatist movements.

I vaguely remember the early morning exercises, the constant and never-ending line-ups for marches, and the dinners in the town of Móstoles with fellow soldiers who shared packages of food sent by our families so we wouldn't go hungry. I can't remember anything else. Absolutely nothing more. I thought about the girlfriend I left behind in Madrid and her luscious lips. To relieve my restrained passion, I wrote long love letters in which I had nothing to say about my monotonous days. When basic training ended, they sent me to the Ministry of the Army located in the Plaza de la Cibeles in Madrid. They assigned me the position of master armorer. My mission was to make sure the Mauser rifles we marched with were kept clean. Once a week I'd distribute them to the troops of our battalion so they could remove whatever flecks of dust had settled on them during the week. I did this routine every seven days. The rest? I don't know. Luckily, there was a mess hall on the first floor of the army building where I got together with some soldiers who were chess fanatics, and we'd play long matches that kept me entertained. I organized classes for illiterate soldiers, and there were quite a few, but I didn't make much progress with my students because the recruits would get reassigned to other battalions and my work would come to a halt. My day at the Army quarters ended at three o'clock in the afternoon. From there, I'd go to my house, change clothes and head for the office to put in a few hours so I could justify the salary they gave me. At night, I attended an academy to continue my studies. I suffered from exhaustion and lack of sleep. I was always sleepy. I barely slept and my young body objected. I remember that I was able to sleep while standing in formation during roll call. I'm not sure if that's true, but I'll mention it anyway because I believe it really happened. At night, there was a lot of homosexual activity, probably because of the repression. The sergeant of our company, Vicente López López, asked me to tutor him in classes for the high school program in which he'd enrolled. A nearly impossible mission because he was stupid and dense. I was arrested several times for ridiculous reasons, for a smudge on the tip of my boots, or for escaping before the official quitting time. I can't remember much more. Little warrior ardor and quite a bit of unjustified waste of time. Franco's army was a gigantic machine with vast numbers, but technically primitive, with many generals who were mediocre in terms of intellect and skillset, which justified the need for more soldiers. It was a dark world of dinosaurs parading around and saluting with the hand on the temple.

My father-in-law, whom I met many years later, was a Colonel in the U.S. Army. That army was completely different because since its independence, it's been involved in one armed conflict after another, or war. Even at 96 years of age, he still liked to be addressed as Colonel John Jay Douglass. He loved the army more than anything else. He received a law degree after serving the army for twenty years. He switched gears and started teaching and eventually became the Dean of the National Attorney School, and a professor of law at the University of Houston. He used to tell me that compared to the army, civilian life was disorganized and inefficient. In his opinion, nothing functioned with the smoothness and effectiveness of military life. I understand that. Blind obedience to superiors facilitates making decisions and carrying them out. There are no disagreements or arguments. At your service, onward and upward. He wanted the world to operate under those same conditions. His army, the U.S. Army, was a well-greased machine with a cause and a purpose, something you must recognize even if you don't agree at all with its mission, which is the way I feel. There's no comparison between that army and the Spanish army of 1964, when I endured my sad and uninspiring military service. I regret not having more humorous and entertaining tales to tell.

I look again at the photo of my father that hangs in the study of my house. It was taken during the Civil War and he's in uniform standing next to my Uncle Ignacio. I keep coming back to the same questions about what military actions they might have carried out as soldiers. They chose to join the winning side. After the war ended, did they have to sign up for three more years of military service? Did they fulfill them? Where? When I get to this point, everything becomes fuzzy. My mother didn't speak much about the subject. When she did, it was to say that her brother, who was a captain in the Republican Army, was imprisoned and condemned to death. But my father and my uncle? When my family, my aunts, that is my father's sisters, spoke about my father, they didn't mention his talents or deeds, but rather his virtues. They would always say that Mariano was very good, a good and honest man at heart. And that's where the story ends, no matter how hard I try to rewrite it.

51

When my brother Mariano turned fifteen, he bought a bicycle with tips he'd saved while working for a distributor
of Mexican films as an errand boy. It created quite a stir in
our house. It was a cheap bike, red, with racing handlebars
and three speeds. The bike was an injection of euphoria for
us because it represented a feeling of freedom, albeit symbolic. We could go to the Parque del Oeste in five minutes
and from there to the university campus where we brothers celebrated our own Olympic cycling races. Because we
only had one bicycle, one of us pedaled while the other sat
on the handlebars. On the university campus, we timed our
races by categories: long distance, middle distance, uphill
and downhill. Other times, I'd take my younger brother,
José Luis, on Sunday adventures on that red bicycle. One
time, on our way home from the park at la Casa del Campo,
my brakes failed at a stoplight and with no way to stop my
frenetic charge, I crashed into a woman crossing the street,
who ended up falling into a puddle. The furious husband of
the battered victim stopped himself from pounding me with
his raised arm and instead, unleashed his fury by grabbing
me by the shoulder and leading me at a brisk pace to the
nearest police station to receive the appropriate punishment.
The officer on duty performed his due diligence and called
my mother, who came to get me and take me home, but not
before giving me a severe scolding. Nothing else came of the
incident except that we had to fix the brakes on the bicycle.

My mother told us that for their honeymoon, they spent two nights at a hotel on the outskirts of Madrid and during the day explored the surroundings and visited places on a rented tandem bicycle. I wonder what Madrid was like in 1941. The war had ended on April 1, 1939. The city had been bombarded systematically for three years to break down the resistance of the Republican government. Madrid was bombed for the first time on August 27 and 28, 1936. In fact, the capital became the first large European city to ever be bombed by airplanes. Franco, the leader of the rebel troops, had declared he'd destroy Madrid before leaving it to the Marxists. To a certain point, he did just that. Hundreds of buildings fell. My grandparents' house, in the Plaza of Moncloa, came down in one of the first bomb raids and the family had to move, leaving everything but the clothes on their backs. They went to Aranjuez, to the home of some friends, where they survived by stealing cabbages and other vegetables from gardens on the shores of the Tajo River.

I wonder what marriage was like and how love flourished in a devastated city, especially for my parents who, after getting married, moved to an apartment in the northern part of the city, which had been one of the most heavily bombed areas. They had to skirt rubble to get to the market, cooking what they could with their rationed provisions. Their only entertainment was the walks they took on Sundays, taking care not to step on live shells or shrapnel. They conceived children and kept silent while listening to the radio propagate the great campaign to honor the heroes and the dead. Perhaps for this reason they went no further than the outskirts of the city for their honeymoon, riding around on a bicycle. Perhaps my passion for cycling comes from that long ago trip.

When Federico Martín Bahamontes won his first Tour de France in 1959, my love of cycling grew. After returning from my Sunday outings cycling in the hills around El Pardo, I'd clip photos from the newspaper of the elite cyclists (Jacque Anquetil, Charly Gaul, Felice Gimondi, Eddie Merckx) and glue them into a scrapbook. Many times, I rode the eleven miles from our house in the Barrio Argüelles to the mountain top of Cristo del Pardo, enjoying those excursions of beautiful youth. Last summer, during a family beach vacation, I repeated that cycling adventure by riding along the bay on the coast of North Carolina, accompanied by my son Philip, my daughter Camila, and my niece Alicia. Maybe I've passed on my passion for cycling to them, maybe not. My father and I never rode bikes together, nor did we climb mountains, or read his favorite poems or my poetry. I never showed him my children or my grandchildren or took him around my university. Nor did we sit down to talk about the tough times in which he lived. I don't know if he hears me. So many years have passed. My new bike is also red, but this one has a frame made of carbon and high-tech components with eighteen speeds and electric brakes. What would my brother's old bicycle, which gave us so many hours of delight, have to say to my current bike, so sleek, sophisticated, and light as a feather?

Today's cities seem to embrace policies that favor travel by bicycle and motorcycles. There are many advantages to cycling. Bicycles are simple and don't require gasoline, oil, or motors that pollute the air. They provide physical exercise and allow us return to a lifestyle in which the body convenes with the landscape. Although I have two cars parked in my driveway, my bicycle continues to be my favorite mode of transportation, as if its red and white frame were a striped peppermint candy. I think I once wrote a poem that began with that verse.

52

Over time, memory gets crusty making it hard to untangle the accumulation of sensations, emotions, impressions, and past experiences. At times, our mind frees us from certain memories, but others persist, leaving us with a sinking feeling. On the morning of November 20, 1975, Spain awakened as on any cold autumn morning, but with a level of anxiety one hundred decibels higher. Many Spaniards had suffered from insomnia the night before in anticipation of what was transpiring. Never before had such a tragic event been accompanied by such hope and happiness. Had the dictator truly died in his bed at the Hospital de la Paz in Madrid? The newspapers that supported the regime were prepared for the tragedy and published the news. Minds struggled to celebrate an inner joy without letting it erupt into hysterical jubilation. The dictator had succumbed after keeping the country in mourning for thirty-nine long years. How could we express our feelings? Whom could we call to share our emotions?

A new phase had begun, and it was time to start the work of rebuilding the country and the constitution. Spain needed to take advantage of the moment. We were all faced with the huge task of creating a democracy in a country with little experience in such matters. According to the "Democracy Index," a recent study conducted by the Intelligence Unit of the United Kingdom in 2018, of 167 countries included in the survey, only twenty fulfilled the requirements to be classified as "Full Democracies." Among them, Spain was number 19. Another fifty-four countries were classified as "Flawed Democracies." It's no surprise that under Trump, the United States appears on that second list. Of the 167 countries, thirty-eight were considered hybrid regimes and fifty-two qualified as authoritarian governments.

Spain's experience with democracy was practically nil, except for five tumultuous years of democratic life between 1931 and 1936, which ended with a military takeover and a bloody Civil War. Before that, the negotiated democracy during the Restoration Period had been limited and inadequate. Democracy is a rare bird that leads a fragile and uncertain life. Like romantic relationships, it must be treated daily with care. It's not enough to make a formal declaration, pray to God on your knees and await good fortune. Democracy must be nourished, pampered, and spoken to every day. Democracy requires patience, understanding, vigilance, daily dialogue, empathy, and the conviction that it's a collective enterprise with no winners or losers.

After that November of 1975, a new constitution was approved in 1978, and Spain experienced three years of uncertainty that were like a courtship. After the scare of the attempted military takeover of Colonel Tejero in 1981, it appeared there would be a wedding and the marriage would last. With each passing day it was obvious the country was changing.

Social norms became more relaxed, and couples could live together. The freedom gave way to all kinds of spontaneous excesses after so many years of repression. We had no model to follow. We could imitate the experiences of France, England, and Holland, observed by many Spaniards who travelled to those neighboring countries, but tourism does little more than provide moments to be captured in photographs. Spain had no democratic tradition. We had to learn how to proceed one step at a time. Censorship disappeared and along with that, the obstacles to creativity. We no longer needed to look over our shoulder to see who was watching or what punishment awaited us. Everything was new and people were free to experiment and engage in activities, some wholesome and others risky and adventurous. It was time to recover happiness and the peace of mind that justice was for all, regardless of religious, political, and civic beliefs.

Like a kid wearing new birthday shoes, I went to vote for the first time in my life on June 15, 1977. The emotion I felt was indescribable. My eyes filled with tears, and I ran to the house to tell Carrie that I'd voted. I'd exercised my rights and felt that Uncle Pepe's imprisonment after the war and the exile of so many Spaniards had not been in vain. Nor had the courageous protests of my friends and fellow students, who'd been corralled or arrested in the streets during so many anti-government manifestations, fallen on deaf ears. Then I remembered my parents and their struggle to escape poverty during those years of hunger that followed the Civil War. I remembered my grandfather Antonio's blue eyes, so honest and sad, eyes that had witnessed the destruction of the Republican party. I'm not sure if my mother celebrated the new freedom or not. By then, the need to make ends meet outweighed political concerns. The last years of the Franco regime had transpired with a certain amount of tranquility or calmness. The economic recovery at the end of the 1960s had eased the strain on the pocketbook. After his death, people continued to repeat the old refrain "with Franco, we lived better," but we didn't live better under him because at times we merely existed. Corruption during the final decades before Franco's death ran rampant, and censorship left a nation of handicapped citizens, without parents or literary and artistic masters. What happened since the return of democracy must be told with the confidence of a gambler who, after placing a large bet and risking everything, came out unscathed. It should be told with the hope that our children will inherit something, if only our ability to compromise and believe that the will of all the people deserves to be respected and accepted.

53

I'm sitting in a little park in Arlington with my four-year-old granddaughter Austen. A child's world puts us in touch with a minimalist reality, a universe of things that seem impossible and imperceptible but are as real as those of the adult world. She picks up acorns and chestnuts from the ground and puts them in a pile with little stones and pieces of tree branches, speaking to them all the while and breathing life into them. She erects a miniscule planet with them. Sitting on a metal bench, I observe her, barely taking notice of the lush trees around me. Then she picks up a ladybug, and both of us look at it for what seems an eternity. Austen marvels at those tiny things, names them, shows them to me and asks questions that barely have an answer because it's hard to make sense of her incoherent pronunciation, or because I feel incapable of understanding her logic. For her, everything has all the sense in the world, in her world, that of a four-year-old child who wakes up every day to wondrous discoveries that never end. Her presence is a constant lesson for me. While I'm with her, I stop looking at my watch and become less obsessed with my to-do list and the passage of time. In this way she teaches me to observe how green the leaves are, how far the branches extend, and to notice the invisible mist in the air and other hidden miracles.

She suggests we play a game. I'm not sure which one, but I watch her as I hide behind a tree. She comes over, finds me, laughs, and runs to the other side of the park, trips, and shakes it off. It's just a game and you must laugh. We stop, she sits down, calls me, and proposes we play a different game with a big ball. It's like a planet spinning in her hands and bouncing across the grass. I try to remember the childhood years of my children, who are all grown up now. I can remember certain sentences they uttered but not the scent of their bodies, the warmth of their gazes, the sweetness of their voices, or the expectation of that next moment that won't be like the one before, but a unique experience marked by the slow passage of time.

LETTER TO MY LITTLE GIRL

Dear child: I am writing
to say I want nothing more
than your soft lingering perfume,
imperfect perhaps, but exquisite,
that ensuing aroma of fresh leaves
and dewy stalks, that fragrance of life,
the breath of childhood worlds,
worlds of fairies and unicorns.

I tell you this, my tiny beloved
two-year-old, for you to know and record
in your infallible diary of memories
that mine is not a heart shielded by
a hero's armor, but a tiny woven box
where I keep children's tears,
along with singing cicadas and crickets,
a place where swans
and dragons gather
to declare love and shed tears.

Things might happen, I say, oh what terrible things,
what other horrible games of iron and brass
could smother the innocence of this dialogue.
Sadly, we must watch out
for the vampire
who snatches bloody kisses
from the warm sands of young girls' lips.

(From *¿Quién eres tú Betty Blue?/*
Who are You Betty Blue?)

54

I've lived in many cities, some for extended periods of time. Cities can exert an influence, like the people who live with us and share our sorrows. The city, with its streets and inhabitants, shops and taverns, aromas and colors, impacts us in a much more intense way than we can imagine. They say pets, especially dogs, resemble their owners. The same thing happens with cities. Their climate, altitude, vegetation, sounds, buildings, and cultural night life affect our bodies and connect us to our surroundings.

I was born in Madrid. We don't ask what the city in which we're born and raised is like, at least not until we reach a certain age, and have moved on and can compare it to other places. Madrid, for me, was Madrid, neither rich nor poor. A city with streets and apartment buildings, with a constant hustle and bustle, street cars and corner shops, lots of bars and theaters, large parks, and a mountain range whose snow-covered peaks loomed like a backdrop in winter. Oftentimes, people who live in the city where they were born rarely visit its museums or get to know its charming sights. They stick to their neighborhoods as if the world consisted of that limited parcel of houses and familiar stores. People from Madrid have never wondered much about their city, a metropolis that expanded under the shadow of political power, the monarchy, and the noble class. That's why it has so many palaces and grandiose buildings and mansions, and monuments that celebrate its imperial history. Unfortunately, it has no access to the sea, only a languishing river whose waters once enriched orchards along its shores but have long since been redirected into channels. As the mother of Bernarda Alba says in García Lorca's tragedy, it's a city of wells. The surrounding mountain range keeps it cool and provides fresh air. The climate is cold in the winter and very hot in the summer.

The Barrio Argüelles, where I grew up, borders the large university campus and the lush Parque del Oeste, spaces engraved on my senses from my childhood and adolescent days – the aroma of honeysuckle and the smell of fried food coming from the taverns. Madrid was the home of my school, church, house, the back courtyard with its mulberry trees, and the busy sidewalks of my neighborhood. It wasn't better or worse than any other city. It was what it was and nothing more. This was the place of my birth and that of my siblings. The original matrix. My prison cell and the site of my early adventures. I never wondered why its river carried so little water or why the sea was so far away or why the sky was always so blue. Nor did I wonder why there were so few automobiles or why there were so many brazen pigeons. Who built its boulevards and parks? Who erected the many ornate gates that once guarded the city when it was protected by walls? It's the city that was illuminated at Christmastime, where people celebrated the season in the decorated Plaza Mayor, dipping churros into hot chocolate. I lived in Madrid until I was twenty-five years old, when for personal reasons, namely my first and only failed marriage, I decided to move to Barcelona, although I also considered London and Lima. Don't ask me why.

The Madrid of my Childhood

In the shadows of thistle and whitewashed walls,
I built my childhood.
I never knew what king, warrior, or dynasty
erected its palaces and crowned its avenues.
What edict, mayor, or architect
designed its boulevards and sowed its gardens.

All of Madrid was an open plaza for wandering,
and the Parque del Oeste rose to contemplate
the arid sea of Castille.

Grandeur of the simple,
of things never recorded,
city of carousel horses from a childhood
preserved in limbo,
where streets are christened with names
and dates commemorated.

On the corner, an entryway to apartments without an elevator
for souls to ascend, a street number,
an entrance, a corridor, a door with a knocker
and the perennial welcome of the mother
at sundown, when windows
reflect the setting sun
and evening music ushers in sleep.

City of my childhood that slumbers and throbs,
whether thirsty or doused by a river
that, in the afternoon, caresses the mimosa trees
with its sweet saliva.

Oh, city of my memory where the present shrinks
and yesterday languishes as timeless as a fairy tale.

(From *Ciudades de tiza. Paisajes de papel/
Chalk Cities. Paper Landscapes*)

That's how Madrid was and still is in my memory. Barcelona evokes another luminous phase of my life. Barcelona, not necessarily all of Catalonia, represents the Mediterranean and a culture devoted to the sea, from the time the first voyageurs set sail from its welcoming shores. The culture of Barcelona developed along those shores, while its political ties kept it tethered to the rest of Spain. The blue swells of water are easier to navigate than waves of mountains, ranges, hills, and rivers of an interior sea. The Levantine coastline became populated after centuries of commerce and conflicts with Phoenicia, Greece, Rome, Turkey, Tunisia, and deep Africa, cultures that left their mark on dwellings, markets, and plazas. In the thirteenth century, Jaume I continued that expansive wave and raised flags in Valencia, the Balearic isles, and Italy.

Barcelona opened the doors of Europe to me. Its proximity to centuries of history called out to me, giving free rein to my youthful desire for adventure and injecting my legs with energy. With a brand-new passport and a rundown Renault 4x4, I traveled constantly to France to buy books, see films, and climb mountains. England beckoned me with its theater, culture, and amazing eccentric architecture. I made other trips to Switzerland, Germany, Austria, and countries behind the Iron Curtain. During the summers, I climbed the highest peaks of the Alps and traveled by boat to the Mediterranean ports of Italy, Greece and its islands. The journey was my inspiration, instigator, and leitmotif. It was the source, the new frontier, and enticing otherness, which presented a constant challenge to my energy, habits, and finances. I made a lot of errors and took so many risks. I said yes to nearly everything that came my way: new jobs, baseless love affairs with no substance, and experiences in acting, writing poetry, and mountain climbing. All this nourished my stifled youth, which flourished with each journey like a lizard shedding its skin of the Catholic beliefs and Spanish political doctrines ingrained in my high school and university education. The strategy was to break with tradition, and the tactic I used was to do so without thinking.

Those were the years I spent studying at the university, still under the aegis of an authoritarian regime, but with enough freedom to embrace European history, literature, philosophical thought, and the latest theories. Years of communal living. Accustomed to living in a tight and loving family circle, in Barcelona, I shared a house, room, kitchen, and social life with a group of friends my age. It was a crazy but fascinating experience. Our close-knit group revolved around our emotional needs. Necessity is a great motivator. We loved, embraced, and helped each other, and played as if our childhood had been extended and we wished to cut loose without the restraints of maturity.

I took on the unimaginable feat of starting a business school, with absolutely no preparation, solving problems as they arose each day and tackling the experience with great optimism. Fortune, if you can call it that, put me in touch with an extraordinary man, José María Boter Quesada. When I speak about him or remember him, he still amazes and fascinates me. He taught me many things and basically helped me to mature because he believed in me. I met him by chance, at the same time I met Carrie, my wife of more than forty years. Without knowing much at all about me, he invited me to start a business school with him. We didn't have money, a place for it, or any kind of official backing. With a university degree in philosophy and literature, I didn't know anything about business. With years as a salesman under his belt, he didn't know that much about starting a business school either. He'd competed in a television program that selected the best salesperson of the year. For the final challenge, the two remaining contestants were given a one thousand pesetas bill to sell and make a profit. José María auctioned his bill off with a famous signature and won. It would be too long and possibly boring to explain how we managed to keep our educational enterprise afloat. The thing is, in less than four years, we had created a fabulous business school, the Management School of Barcelona, which offered a master's in management, with classes during the morning, afternoon, and night. He was the General Manager, and I was the Director of Studies, in charge of the curriculum and hiring instructors. In practice, we did everything together and never had an argument, although his excessive use of shifty dealings shocked me. We tried to model our business school after those in the United States. Such an undertaking, during the last years of Franco's rule and the beginning of the Transition Period, seemed an attractive and unusual novelty.

In Management School, I met Carrie, whom we hired as an English teacher. Soon we went out on our first dates to jazz concerts in the Palau de la Música and trips to the Pyrenees and the Picos de Europa in Asturias. It was Carrie who spoke of her need to pursue graduate studies and urged me to do the same. My career at the university in Barcelona had left me with a feeling of dissatisfaction not compensated by the money I made at our business school. And so, without delay, after making the decision to apply for graduate school, we sold the few possessions we had, our two cars, her SEAT 600 and my SIMCA 1200, and took a plane to JFK in New York City, and from there to Houston. That was the beginning of the American phase of our lives. We thought that after completing our graduate studies, we'd return to Spain. But that didn't happen. Nor did we know where we'd end up, or what we'd study. Life, the unstoppable force of life took charge and guided our steps, which were many, and applauded our successes, which were many as well. Along the way, there were setbacks and crises. It wouldn't be life without them. We managed as best we could. Carrie very well, with that ironfisted will of hers. I, being more spontaneous, carried on believing that eventually we'd land safely. What we didn't know was that the next city to take us in would become a witness to a story that has lasted forty years, Charlottesville.

55

I threw myself into the unknown and landed in a sea of grass. Virginia is essentially green. From the Atlantic coast, it traverses vast forests and fields, crossing the Appalachian Mountains, all the way to the Ohio River. It rains constantly. Winters are mild, springs blossom, summers are hot and humid, and autumn is a delight for the senses. Adapting wasn't easy for me. The language barrier is hard to overcome, especially for someone trying to learn a new language after turning thirty. Charlottesville is a university town. Its buildings and monuments are modeled after Thomas Jefferson's original design. He's the emblematic figure and founding father behind the creation of the university, the one who designed its architecture and served as its first chancellor.

Shortly after arriving, I began my studies when I could barely speak the language. Whenever I talk about my life in America to my friends in other parts of the world, I can't help but speak about my experience in the university, which is my house, my home, my place of work and play, my refuge, my source of inspiration, my daily dialogue, my temple. Every day I walk from my house and cross the campus to my office or the libraries. I get the feeling I'm living in a twenty-first century monastery, an institution completely devoted to teaching and research in equal measure.

That monastic character that I attribute to this place is tempered by the constant presence of sports. In the United States sports are perfectly integrated into high schools and universities for several reasons. First, they foster and develop discipline and habits relevant to life. Secondly, sports preserve emotional ties with the institution for its former students. Alumni attend football and basketball games and relive their schooldays, remember their years in the classroom, and donate to the university coffers. I don't believe this practice was initiated by monks because the university never had any, although it still seems like a monastery to me. It's a secular institution, with a chapel in the middle of campus open to all creeds and non-religious activities. This university is where I studied, learned to conduct research with discipline, and to write. I was surrounded by renowned academicians and scholars who encouraged and motivated me. The solitude of this provincial city invites withdrawal, unlike Spain with its distracting bars and street life. Here you bury yourself in the halls of the library, or in the home office, in pursuit of intellectual endeavors.

My children Philip, Peter, and Camila were born here. I had no option but to learn to be a father. Though I wasn't the best husband, I was a decent dad. I enjoyed my children and suffered with them and because of them. I watched them grow up while we played soccer, rode bicycles, and climbed up and down mountains. I watched them go to high school, stumble through the quagmire of youth, and navigate their college years. I tried to pass on my pleasures and passions, and in many ways, I was successful.

Over time, I've become one with the landscape that was hostile to me at first. I'm not sure how much of a Virginian exists in me. At a certain age, the skin thickens and protects you against foreign influences and the tyranny of passions. But Charlottesville for me is home, my home, the land where I'll be laid to rest when my time comes.

There's another city that I feel close to personally and professionally, Valencia, where I've spent many months, maybe years counting my frequent long visits there. I made my first trip in 1982 to get to know the university and set up an exchange program for students and academic interchanges, with the help of Enrique Celma and his family, who are generous to a fault. The negotiations flourished and as a result, thousands of North American students have enjoyed a cultural and educational experience in the city by the Turia River. I achieved this with the cooperation of brilliant minds. I was able to spend prolonged periods there and got to know the region and its celebrations, and people with whom I've enjoyed long-lasting relationships. There are few cities in which I feel more at home than I do in Valencia. Some of my best friends live there and welcome me with open arms each time I visit, as if I were a prodigal son. Valencia is a luminous city with a special passion for fire. It takes you under its wing and embraces the enriching circles of life.

I've spent many seasons in other cities that I know very well, such as Washington, D.C., New York City, Houston, Buenos Aires, and Resistencia. Does that make me a citizen of the world? I've had the good fortune to travel for years as a tourist and have embarked on grand journeys. Possibly the voyage that has impacted me most of all the journeys I've experienced over the years, because of its scope and numerous stimuli, was a trip I took around the world on a ship in 2010, in the company of my wife Carrie and my dear friend David T. Gies. We were invited to be part of an academic team on a program called Semester at Sea. The premise is that a ship with the capacity to hold two thousand people sails around the world for four academic months, while professors teach classes and discuss topics related to conservation, energy, pollution, and production and distribution of resources. It took me more than a year to digest that four-month experience spent sleeping in a fishbowl, observing its fluvial motion, basking in the warm afternoons at sea, or greeting the new day each morning as waves crashed against the hull and splashed the balcony of our cabin. The arrival to a port was always met with great excitement. While the ship made its way to harbor, the early morning light illuminated the city, the one never seen, perhaps never imagined, the city rising at the ocean's shore, with seabirds darting in the skies and the smell of seaweed in the air. We had no expectations and no one waiting for us. Once in the port, we ventured into its streets, jungles, or roads with the passion of explorers. We knew we'd encounter new experiences tinged with curiosity and ignited by the scenery the new country offered us. We embarked on August 23, 2010, from Virginia Beach and returned to San Diego, California, four months later, after having circled the planet, gaining upon our return, one extra day of life from the calendar. That's when I became more aware of the magnitude of our terrestrial globe and its expansive seas.

RETURNING TO LAND

Upon returning, like a lamp
shining bright to greet you,
the arms of the shore open wide
like a father awaiting
his seafaring son.

In San Diego, the ocean quells
the unrelenting vigor of its white tongue,

whose voice clamors from the bowels of the sea,
knocking tenaciously at the door.

I forge the bays, it says,
I encircle the isles,
and thrum the rocks,
lest the land fall asleep,
and the meandering foot
forget the misty silhouette of steel.

Time will tell where I laid my head,
what mounts I rode,
and in what land
my wayfaring foot took root and came to rest.

I'm returning to land.

> (From *La vuelta al mundo en 80 poemas/
> Around the World in 80 Poems*)

56

It was on my bucket list to travel the Road to Santiago. I'm not sure if it was a challenge or a ritual. I called Vicente, my adventurous Valencian buddy, and off we went. In the Abbey of Roncesvalles, where we registered and picked up a passport to be stamped in the churches and inns we'd pass, I had to provide the reason for making the journey. I marked "sport" in the little box. It certainly wasn't for sightseeing, although my camera did record the pilgrimage. There was a little box for "spiritual" reasons. That wasn't my case either. The heart of the medieval towns, the tranquility of the landscape, and the lure of green were better reasons.

Once the journey begins, the hours pass without a watch or clock, and time is measured by a stone in the road, the bountiful countryside, the serenity of the clouds, a well-earned fatigue, and inner peace. Pilgrims flee Paris in October and celebrate the energy that lingers in their old age. They are light amidst so much darkness. The Peruvian poet César Vallejo once wrote: "I will die in Paris under a downpour/ on a day I already remember/ I will die in Paris – and stand my ground – / perhaps on a Thursday, like today, in autumn." The world is divided into those who celebrate life and those who mourn death. I feel the emotion of one who embraces life, who gazes at the night sky and revels under the glorious stars. I'll wear myself out pedaling without counting the days as they go by. If time stops at some point, this is the moment. At the crossroad, I witness the miracle.

In Puente de la Reina emotion transformed into weariness. Isn't that the way life is? The pebbles on the road, humble or indifferent, offer themselves to the foot, as the Spanish poet León Felipe suggests: "Like you, little stone; like you, I love that you tumble along streets and sidewalks; like you, humble pebble of the road; like you." The simplest things are what move me the most. There is no sea along the road to Santiago, only the triumph of the land, the glory of the plains, and the flaming ardor of ochre and green. I don't know how many blisters I must endure to appreciate the extent of my adventure.

In El Burgo Ranero, a godforsaken town, only God knows which god, pilgrims who found lodging in hostels and inns shared the highlights of the day's journey over glasses of wine. Some followed a straight route, others a winding one of pebbles and rocks, but everyone headed in the same direction on the road to Santiago. For Vicente and me, the days were long, seven or eight hours of cycling. We'd stop here and there to get something to drink and stock up on provisions to fill our stomachs. You must keep your strength up. During those brief stops, we'd engage in conversation with other travelers dotting the route like tiny ants in search of an opening. The tone was fraternal, the greeting simple *buen camino*, an expression we used to identify ourselves as fellow pilgrims and express our sincere wishes. The road is the typical metaphor for life, a route toward a destiny we can't foresee. After greeting hundreds of pilgrims whom we met along the way and wishing them *buen camino*, we wondered about those in the world who didn't embrace the greeting.

We spent a week biking across the territory of Northern Spain. When you cover so many kilometers, everything takes on a new dimension. After a good night's sleep and breakfast, a breeze announced the new day and the long distance ahead.

We rode, enjoying the mild morning and crisp colors of the landscape. After two hours, we took a break and ate a wedge of tortilla de patata, downing it with fruit juice. Vicente and I studied the map, calculating how many kilometers and legs of the trip were left. On the first few days, we stopped to have lunch. We were always hungry. In Rabanal del Camino, a lovely village in the province of León, near Galicia, they offered us *cocido maragato*, a very heavy version of the *cocido madrileño*, a traditional stew from Madrid. After a few days, we realized it was better not to take long breaks because they made it harder to get back in the rhythm. Not to mention that some evenings we arrived very late to our destination, like when we made it to Castrogeriz, a medieval town we only caught a glimpse of because it was so dark, and we were so tired that we just wanted to climb into bed and not move. There was no time to look around, write, or read. Most of my thoughts vanished as I navigated the gravel on the road, so I focused on the scenery. Harvested fields glistened like gold and church towers shone brightly under the morning sun. There was a daily threat of rain and storms, but we didn't get wet until the last leg of the journey. Climbing the steep hills to O Cebreiro, we got caught in a downpour that lasted twenty minutes. As soon as we made it to our next stop and took refuge, the storm really let loose. We felt sorry for the pilgrims arriving on foot completely soaked. For the most part, the pilgrims were foreigners in their fifties, or older. There were French, German, and Dutch pilgrims and young North American girls with blond braids, a few Asian walkers, and groups of rowdy Spaniards.

I think about the road and how it brings so many people together. I wonder how many Christians make the pilgrimage for religious reasons. If they're believers, how many truly believe in the myth of Santiago, Christ's disciple who came to this peninsula to preach the gospel. After long and fruitless journeys, he ended up being sacrificed in Jerusalem, and his disciples brought his remains to Galicia and buried them there. Historically speaking, it's an improbable legend, only believable for those who have faith. Faith is the great equalizer; it justifies all, challenges science and reason, and erects the framework needed to sustain beliefs and support our fragile humanity. It's the same faith that drives us to pursue our fleeting destiny on this earth and satisfy our need to leave something behind in the wake of our footsteps. The faith that leads us to put a stone in our backpack and take it to Cruz de Fierro, the faith that helps us cross the sea or climb a mountain, a faith without age, time, months, or heavy sorrow. We want to leave something behind and that's why we have children and celebrate holidays. We undertake impossible tasks that allow us to leave a trace of ourselves. We think that someone will remember them, maybe even write about them in a notebook that will silently gather dust.

O Cebreiro rises like a simple fort beneath a cloudy sky. Its streets are lined with houses, surrounded by stone walls that continue all the way to the valley, winding into green fields. Getting to this point is quite the feat if you're traveling by bicycle, with saddlebags and a backpack of equal weight. You must keep peddling because any hesitation can be a setback, and you must pay close attention to the curves in the road, especially in the fog. We arrived with the excitement of runners nearing the finish line, but with no one present to cheer us on; only the exquisite reward of a long rest. We looked at each other to share a moment of silence and the satisfaction of knowing the end was in sight. The same excitement could be felt in the hostels and inns where pilgrims stretched their tired legs and exchanged complicit looks of contentment. I made it there too. It's not always that way. Some bodies give in to the demands of the route. That's the way life is too. It's a matter of when, how, and where. It rained the whole way from Palas de Rei to Santiago, a day of christening, or perhaps an act of purification before entering the cathedral. Accompanied by God or not, the mounting emotion with each day of the journey made the arrival to Santiago exhilarating. I don't know how many blessings we earned on that trip that would provide us entrance to some heaven, somewhere. For me, paradise is right here, and I cling to it, without haste, to keep from forgetting to enjoy each day. As John Lennon once said, "Life is what happens to you while you're busy making other plans."

> Like a stroke of ink in the dark,
> like a violin with no melody,
> I cross the terrain of this land
> of pilgrims traveling to Santiago.
> Within my chest
> uncertainty spins
> like the spokes of my windmill,
> like my restless bicycle,
> like the hands of the clocktower.

> It is the twilight hour.

> It is my blissful weariness.

> It is el Camino.

(From *Pureza demolida/
Ravaged Purity*)

57

As a child, your father seems like a rock. If that rock shatters, the pieces scatter and can't easily be put back together. There were four of us kids, of different ages. My sister Lourdes was a romantic at heart, a cheerful blond, but near the end of her life she became sad. Her smile disappeared from her lips for a long time. Years before, when my father died, she helped manage the house and turned to love for an escape. Marcelo was the first boyfriend, and the second, Joaquín, who became her husband a few years later. He was tall, refined, and had an air of confidence that attracted her. She married very young and was happy raising four beautiful children, but hated household chores, especially cooking and catering to her very demanding husband who was impossible to please. She tried as best she could, never giving up. More than one tear was shed, casting a shadow over her blue eyes. She didn't attend college, although with her intuitive knowledge and vivid imagination, she'd have been a brilliant student. Her three daughters, Laura, Sylvia, and Alicia did earn university degrees. Her son, Javier, slipped into a black hole but finally managed to climb out of it and did well for himself. Landmark years passed around that time. It was the period when Spain's universities opened their doors to the struggling middle class. Although Lourdes didn't attend a university, she found refuge in reading, her true passion, and going to the movies on Saturdays with her husband, or to an art gallery, and the much anticipated summer vacations. For her, vacations meant spending the entire summer at the beach, or in the mountains, and renting a house or apartment for several months. When her children grew older and became more independent, her house began to feel too large. She still enjoyed the company of her girlfriends, with whom she shared her most enjoyable pastime, conversation. She'd settle down with a cup of coffee and a cigarette and pose an endless stream of questions. She took an interest in everything, and never settled for a brief response, always probing to learn more. She was a perfect communicator, an expert at the art of dialogue, skilled at keeping the conversation flowing, an art that few people master.

When her husband retired, she wanted to find something enjoyable to do outside the house. For years, she volunteered for a program called "Hombre," which helped the ever-increasing number of drug addicts come clean. She'd talk with the families who'd struggled with that terrible problem in their homes. She felt she was doing something worthwhile, especially during the final years of her life when she began to lose faith. Losing loved ones and friends is difficult, but feeling abandoned by God is another matter, a tragedy without an easy solution. She came to visit us in January of 2005, and stayed in our house in Charlottesville. She attended rehearsals and the debut of the play we put on that year, *Noches de amor efímero* by Paloma Pedrero. One of the actors was her daughter Alicia, the nomad of the family, who'd come to Charlottesville to pursue a doctorate in Spanish literature. Lourdes was moved by the play and cried. She cried easily. One day, she returned from one of her walks around campus with a bloody scratch on her cheek. She said she'd fallen but couldn't remember how or where. It happened a second time. After returning to Madrid, she was examined for a possible illness or depression, and was diagnosed with several brain tumors. She lived until July of that year. She passed away with so much to live for and so many potential plans for what she'd hoped would be a new phase in her life, when she no longer had to change diapers or deal with adolescent crises of those years when happiness is an obligation. She passed away, leaving in the inkwell maternal concerns and unanswered questions as to what she would've liked to be and do with the rest of her life.

58

I don't remember when I began to write poetry. It had to have been at some point. Perhaps in school, or when my father, who was already ill, turned to poetry for solace and asked us to read to him, or at family parties where we'd clamor to recite poems. While fulfilling military service at the Plaza de la Cibeles, news spread that the high command had organized a poetry contest. I imagine they were hoping for patriotic elegies or something like that. The prize was two weeks off from service, which was substantial. I got down to business and wrote a ballad that narrated the tragedy of recruits abandoning their towns and villages to comply with the mandatory draft that took them away from their jobs, loved ones, and homeland. Now that I think about it, it was quite a provocative ballad. As you might surmise, I didn't win. I was lucky they didn't arrest me for defamation of the army's preeminent mission.

After discovering Miguel Hernández and falling in love forever with his poetry, I spent a frenetic period unleashing my feverish poetic passion. I never attended a creative writing workshop for poetry, nor did I read critical studies on poetry that would've pointed me in the right direction. What I did was imitate the poets I liked who wrote in Spanish, or those who wrote in any other language and were translated to Spanish: Paul Eluard, Charles Baudelaire, Arthur Rimbaud, Rudyard Kipling, Emily Dickinson, Walt Whitman, Sylvia Plath, Rabindranath Tagore, Leonard Cohen, Miguel Labordeta,

Nicolás Guillén, Pablo Neruda, and César Vallejo, especially Vallejo whose poems I didn't understand but loved.

I kept writing and gathering poems into collections with titles such as: "The Son is the Third Dimension of your Side," "Verses from My Left Shoulder," and "Rainy Days and Other Stars." I still have them somewhere in the attic of my house. A friend of a friend of mine who lived in Wisconsin printed a handcrafted edition of the last one. Years later, I accompanied Evangelina Rodríguez on a trip to Georgetown on one of her visits to Virginia, and while sitting in a bar telling stories and confiding in each other, I dared to ask her if she'd read a manuscript with poems I'd put together somewhat randomly, a collection that was also lacking a title. She agreed and took it with her when she returned home to Valencia. A few weeks later, I received a handwritten letter in perfect calligraphy, as if it had been printed professionally. She told me she liked the manuscript and was going to publish it in Ardeas, a collection she directed in Sagunto. I was adamant that the volume be illustrated with drawings by a talented artist and former student of mine, Linda Phillips, and she agreed. When I finally got around to thinking about a title, nothing occurred to me. That's when Linda, who'd been working with the poems to create the accompanying drawings, pointed out something I hadn't realized. "You know, she said, "there's a farewell in almost every poem." Obviously, the poems reflected the trauma I'd experienced when I left Spain, my job, my friends, my family, my mountains, and my sky. In the end, the book was published in 1987 with the title *Despedidas* (*Goodbyes*). It includes poems entitled "Nostalgic Monday," "Without a Grip," "Enough," and "Come to My Funeral."

Looking back, I realize poetry has helped me express my feelings and what I didn't know I was feeling. It helped appease my sadness, nostalgia, and loneliness, using language, that marvelous instrument without which we couldn't feel, think, explain, or question ourselves. The publication of *Despedidas* made me realize something I hadn't thought of before, that there existed a possible reader, that what I wrote and spilled onto the page was destined for a potential reader with whom I was communicating in an indirect way, someone in whom I was confiding my sorrows.

As I recall the volumes of poetry that followed, it seems they were part of a learning process. I realized that if I wanted to improve, I needed to ask for help. I don't believe in inspiration. I'll admit that on occasion, inspiration strikes and comes to the rescue, but for the most part, writing poetry is the work of an artisan, or craftsman. As the poet Gabriel Celaya writes, "I feel like I'm an engineer of verses, a laborer." That artisanal work has taken years to learn and sometimes unlearn, as I explore new paths, making wrong turns along the way. I've composed most of my work while living in the United States, a country that, with rare exceptions, doesn't value or promote Hispanic authors. Living here, I'm far removed from the inner circles of poets, publishing houses, and literary prizes. For this reason, I'm indebted to Evangelina Rodríguez for publishing my work and writing several reviews of my books. I also extend my gratitude to Sergio Arlandis for his interest in my books. He read some of my unpublished manuscripts and published poems in several literary magazines. In 2017, he published an impressive volume dedicated to my poetry: *El sujeto y sus aristas. La poesía de Fernando Operé en el mapa político español.* The year before, Manuel Asensi, editor of *Prosopopeya*, dedicated an entire issue of the journal to "La poesía de Fernando Operé."

A primordial aspect of poetry is its orality. In school and at home, we'd often recite poetry. On my mother's birthday,

January 6th, Three Kings Day, the family would gather at our house and, as if it were a grand performance, we'd recite poems for the guests, which we'd memorized. I've always been good at that. I love to recite poems and give dramatic readings of them. I can do so for hours on end. I think the poems are inside me, like seeds growing silently in the subconscious. Sometimes when I'm walking or driving long distances, I recite out loud. In Argentina, I've given recitals on numerous occasions with Mempo, accompanied by piano, accordion, and guitar played by Daniel Moscatelli. We performed in the Guido Theater of Resistencia, in the Chaco, and took our show on the road to different cities and towns across the country: Corrientes, Sáenz Peña, Rafaela, Gualeguaychú, Rosario, Buenos Aires, and others I can't recall. From those experiences, we made two CDs with accompanying books: *Concierto de poesía a dos voces* (2004) and *Cántico Segundo* (2009).

I suppose that after so many years, so many books, and so many poems, the time has come to confront the mystery of what it means to be a poet. I believe there are poets and those who write poetry. To be a poet is to look at the world in a unique way, to gaze upon it with the tools that poetry has to offer. I'm not sure which of the two categories I belong to. What I know for certain is that I'm indebted to those who inspired me: my parents, my siblings, the Hermanos de La Salle who taught me, all the poets whose works I've read and memorized, and the friends who've accompanied me on this journey. Borges once said, "We have the obligation to hope."

59

I remember the faces and names of friends from my childhood and adolescence. I tell my children they're treasures I've gathered over the years. They're the ones who are there when I need them, the ones who shared my adventures and misfortunes, intimate friends with whom we observe the devout practice of loyalty. I've had the good fortune to count on great friends who go all the way back to my first school years. Without them, my life story wouldn't be the same or worth narrating. Without them, it would be like a table missing a leg, or the sky without a rainbow when the sun comes out on a rainy afternoon. My childhood friends were courageous and adventuresome. Maybe that's why I chose them, or they chose me. They were the ones who took the first steps down the risky and mysterious path I chose to travel. I wonder where that innate gregariousness comes from. I don't recall that my father or mother had many friends, at least not intimate friends. Those who attended the parties we had in our house for birthdays, holy days, and Christmas were family – grandparents, uncles, aunts, and brother and sister in-laws – a joyful extended family.

My best childhood friend was Adrián Moure. He was more daring, and I learned a lot from him. I've tried searching his name on the internet but can't find him. When I was fourteen, I met Paco Seco Sánchez-Seco. We sat next to each other at the night school where we earned our high school diplomas. When classes ended, we'd share long conversations as we walked home together until our routes branched off in different directions. We'd talk about everything – our classes, our families, the good and the bad, and who knows what else. We were the best of friends until one day we both fell for the same girl. I was more fortunate and for months kept it a secret. What terrible disloyalty! When I finally revealed my feelings, silence came over our friendship and the distance ruptured what had seemed unbreakable. Today we both have grown children and grandchildren, and although we live continents apart, we celebrate those moments with the joy of the eternal.

Evenings spent under the moon and stars united me with those friends who were also drawn to nature. I've made friends with people wherever I've gone. During the years I studied at the university, I lived in a kind of commune in which four unique individuals forged a friendship in our time of need. Together, we acted in theater, made spontaneous trips, climbed mountains, shared household chores, personal compositions, political ideas, letters and secrets, aspirations, and frustrations. We also weathered storms when it would've been easier to walk away. Aren't such lessons in tolerance the basis for friendship? My annual trips to Madrid, Valencia, Barcelona, Buenos Aires and the Chaco, Kentucky, Massachusetts, Puerto Rico, and Florida are trips made for conversation, with or without words. When I go to Spain, I get together with my friends from Madrid once a year, but they're with me all the other days too. I want them to be part of my life, and they are, as long as they're in my thoughts. Friendship, like love, must be nurtured and encouraged so it doesn't wither away. I have friends whom I admire. They nourish and motivate me and spur me on. Other friends benefit from an injection of my optimism, something innate in my personality.

Those who visit my house, know to come hungry. My mother taught me the ritual of giving, that of filling a plate with lentils and placing it on the table with a generous glass of wine. Feeding others is a one of the most common rituals in every culture, even if later wars are waged. Christians believe the Son of God offered his body to nourish us and keep us from forgetting him. My friend Eliseo Valle dons a pair of rubber gloves, and at his kitchen altar, carries out the ritual of seasoning the dishes he knows I like. He hopes to please me so that the conversation and confidences will blend with the delicious flavors he conjures with his culinary magic. Mempo unsheathes his knife, takes off his shirt, and begins the lengthy process of the Argentine asado, the art of grilling. As the variety of meat change texture and color, he cuts off pieces and serves them to me with a, "how's that?" Meanwhile, he'll offer a few nibbles about his latest novel, although writers are reluctant to reveal such details. After performing heart surgery, Juan Martínez-León employs his meticulous surgical skills to prepare yet another way of serving lamb, which he knows is my favorite meat. I like it when my friends gather in the kitchen when I'm the one officiating the ceremony. For me, that's the great metaphor of life, a public ritual in which nothing is hidden. In this way, we fulfill our obligation to feed the hungry, a form of charity implicit in all religions. With religion or without it, the ritual has the same meaning for believers and atheists alike.

60

We're in the room where my father-in-law John Jay Douglass is dying. A hard transition from this world to the unknown. Neither religions, nor prophets, nor comprehensive scientific studies can catch a glimpse of the grand mystery. What awaits us in the afterlife? At my mother-in-law's funeral, a Episcopalian minister delivered a pleasant and engaging eulogy in which he told us about a book he'd just published on the experiences of people who, after being declared biologically dead, return to life. His findings were optimistic and luminous: a state of material transcendence gives way to weightlessness and light. If that's how it is, I'll sign up, because the steps leading up to that moment are neither pleasant nor enjoyable.

The breath becomes unstable, the pulse races, and the throat struggles for oxygen. The muscles disengage and twitch spontaneously. Oh weary heart whose flowing current dries up in hidden pathways. The Grim Reaper doesn't do us harm intentionally, nor does he show his dark side or scythe. Death is only another phase, another swift passage that can even be a blessing. We humans, the homo sapiens species, have spent some 60,000 years cycling through life and death. We pass on the torch and our genes. We remember what we learned and pass it on so that others will put it to good use, easing their journey. No sooner do we learn that lesson, then it's time to find a replacement to sleep in our bed, read our book, and keep our photos until the day comes when no one recognizes who's in them. That's when oblivion sets in and we cease to exist, even though our DNA travels round and round between those thousands of years that connects the past to the future.

We are here in the present now, and my father-in-law is at death's door, in his bed in the nursing home, clinging for life and gasping for air in the miasma, oblivious to my gaze. I'm not sure why I write these thoughts, or for whom. I think it's my way of giving meaning to my life, a way of praying. I no longer believe what I learned in school or during the years of my Christian fervor, nor does any of that matter to me anymore.

I didn't watch my father die. They brought his dead body home. They laid him out to rest in a Franciscan robe that made him look strange and kept me from getting close to him, as a son should. At her funeral, I contemplated my mother through the opening of a coffin. Her thin face seemed made of wax. This is how we look when the heart stops beating. I look at the body of my exhausted father-in-law and believe his faltering breath will stop at any moment. Then it will be time for goodbyes and memorial services. Meanwhile, my children feed their offspring and tell them stories about their great-grandfather, teaching them the traditions we share so that order isn't undermined, and death can continue opening the door to life.

PRAYERS

Father, how tired you seem to me,
like an old coat
dangling from a hanger.

Son, how tall you look to me.
My meager bones
can't keep up with your height,
or the brusque changes of the century,
or the boleros.

Wife, how shriveled our flesh
feels to the touch.
We seem like two dreary clouds
fading away with a kiss.

House, how fragile your bones.
The illusion of a sturdy home
trickles down the drain,
or are we dreaming like children,
and loving in love.

Mother, we're both old.
You, in your heaven, and I
without a why or a wherefore.

(From *El vigilante*/
The Watchman)

61

I'm in my house in Charlottesville, a week away from the presidential elections in the United States, possibly the most important since the end of World War II. What's at stake is not the election of a president, but democracy. Carrie wakes up anxious each morning, almost in tears. Anxiety is eating away at us little by little. This country, which I admired when I arrived in 1978, has fallen into a state of institutional decomposition that threatens the greatest of its 18th century achievements, the modern representative democracy. Like many great tragedies, it happened right under our noses. I don't believe Trump is aware of the repercussions of his irresponsible political decisions. He lacks the critical capacity and the historic perspective to judge the consequences of his presidential decrees. Under the protection of populist maneuvers, the social fabric of the nation is deteriorating, transforming repeated lies into axioms, and throwing off balance the scales of democracy with decrees from the White House of a clearly authoritarian nature. The sad reality is that one of the two great parties feels threatened by the popular vote, especially that of minorities, and thus uses all the tricks of the trade to ensure the silence of the Black population. This was the same segment of the population silenced after the Civil War in 1867, until 1968, with the so-called Jim Crow laws. These were responsible for reinforcing racial segregation in the south and depriving Black minorities access to presidential and state elections. Slavery ended but not marginalization and alienation.

I think about all those who fought for democracy in Spain during my childhood and university years: the lawyers assassinated in Atocha, the protesters repressed for demanding a more just society, and those incarcerated for expressing their opinions and dissent. I think about the authoritarian Spain in which I grew up, about my father and my mother whose image I see on the faces of my grandchildren, about the impoverished version of democracy we'll hand down to them because of our inability to stand up to corruption. I think about the three marches from Selma to Montgomery in 1965 and their many victims.

What's at stake is much more than the reelection of the most corrupt and incompetent president in the history of the United States, but rather the world with its perennial needs, chronic poverty, widespread hunger, asphyxiating pollution, and global warming. The blue planet is at risk with ulcers that fester as the sky fills up with toxic air and the rivers and seas with detritus. It shouldn't be this way in the 21st century with so many advances in science and technology. The reality is that we've barely noticed that exploiters and dictators have been slipping into power. The Arab Spring didn't produce democratic governments but rather new fanatical figures, imams, and defenders of dark religions. Franco made national Catholicism his rallying cry and transformed it into his political platform. Trump is supported by various denominations of evangelical and fundamentalist churches. For many of his followers, Trump is a savior, although he's never stepped foot inside a church nor attended any type of religious service. If he's a devout worshiper of some religion, it's Trumpism. There's nothing more perverse than creating idols from statues of clay and neon. Trump made it to the presidency by spreading lies, such as the misrepresentation that Barack Obama wasn't born in the United States and therefore was an illegitimate president. He concludes his lamentable presidential term of four years sabotaging the country with accusations of electoral fraud and dragging his twisted lies into court.

Franco submerged the country in darkness during thirty-nine years, but his actions didn't go beyond the borders of the peninsula. The actions of the United States have repercussions throughout the world, and soon, the imitators will appear. Rubén Darío wrote in his poem "To Roosevelt": "The United States is powerful and great / when it quivers a deep quake is felt / passing through the enormous vertebrae of the Andes."

I came to this country in 1978 and I admired, like a child at an amusement park, its democracy that I thought didn't depend entirely on the electoral system, which is always confusing and unequal, but on its people, and the respect they have for each other. Democracy is believing that others have the same rights as you. Today we're witnesses to the subtle shift toward authoritarianism, perhaps the consequence of a slow deterioration of the empire.

Next Tuesday, November 3, 2020, the world, my father in his heaven, the Freedom Fighters of Alabama, my children and grandchildren, my many North American friends, and all those who wish for a world that is more sympathetic and fair, will know the outcome of this threat that has invaded the purest corners, not under the cover of night but in plain daylight, as we enjoy the benefits of the internet, computers, the instant means of communication, and the society of consumerism that has reached an extreme.

And I came to this country to flee the long nightmare of Francoism.

POSTSCRIPT

January 6th, Three Kings Day. In the Hispanic world the Wise Men of the East herald the arrival of gifts they bring children. In Washington, D.C., the gift for this Kings Day has been a violent invasion of the quintessential house of the democratic institution, the Congress of the United States. The eyes of millions of viewers throughout the world are glued to television screens in disbelief. Democracy has been turned upside down. On January 7, 2021, *The New York Times* publishes the following statement: "This is how it ends. The presidency of Donald John Trump, rooted from the beginning in rage, division, and conspiracy, comes to an end with a violent mob assaulting the Capitol, incited by a defeated leader who clings to power as if the United States were just another authoritarian nation." The words to describe yesterday's vandalistic acts could be coup, insurrection, mutiny, sedition. Suddenly, the United States can be compared to a "Banana Republic," which garners concern or receives support from other countries. Like many Spaniards of my generation, this evokes the scene in the Supreme Court of Madrid, on February 23, 1981, when a group of Civil Guards, under the command of Colonel Tejero, attacked the parliamentary building and attempted to put an end to the recently restored democracy. Suddenly, Franco's Spain and Trump's America seem to resemble each other. God help us.

My voice is the voice in the desert, a distant voice that comes from the bitter dictatorship in which I was raised and

313

educated. Mine is an impotent voice that trembles in isolation before a world that's fractured and splitting apart, where authoritarian governments proliferate. I don't know if that's why I wrote this book, so that the echo of my words may reach someone and together we can save the most genuine values of our inheritance as members of democratic communities, which are respect and rights for all.

CITED BOOKS OF POETRY BY FERNANDO OPERÉ:

El vigilante (2022)
La imprudencia de vivir (2018)
Pureza demolida (2017)
Liturgia del atardecer (2016)
Ciudades de tiza. Paisajes de papel (2014)
La vuelta al mundo en 80 poemas (2012)
Cántico segundo (2009)
Anotado al margen. Cuaderno de ruta (2007)
Concierto de poesía a dos voces (2004)
Alfabeto de ausencias (2002)
Salmos de la materia (2000)
Acróbata de ternuras (1994)
¿Quién eres tú Betty Blue? (1991)
Despedidas (1987)

About the Author

Fernando Operé was born in Madrid. He studied at the University of Barcelona and earned a doctoral degree from the University of Virginia. He is a poet and historian, and since 1980 has been a professor at the University of Virginia. He is also a theater director, with a long history of directing plays in Spanish at the University of Virginia. In 2020, he published *Historia de un escenario*, a book that provides an overview of his experiences as a director. He is the author of several books of history, including: *España y las luchas por la modernidad* (2018), *Relatos de cautivos en las Américas desde Canadá a la Patagonia, siglos XVI al XX* (2016), *Indian Captivity in Spanish America: Frontier Narratives* (2008). To date, he has published sixteen books of poetry, including: *No todo será perdonado* (2022); *El vigilante* (2022); *La imprudencia de vivir* (2018); *Pureza demolida* (2017); *Liturgia del atardecer* (2016); and *La vuelta al mundo en 80 poemas/ Around the World in 80 Poems* (2013). His memoir, *En el nombre del padre: crónica de la España de Franco a la América de Trump* (2022) was published in Spain. For more information, please visit: www.operesantillana.com.

About the Translator

Rhonda Dahl Buchanan, Professor Emerita of Spanish at the University of Louisville, has published critical studies and translations of fiction and non-fiction by authors from Latin America and Spain. She received an NEA Literature Fellowship in 2006 for her translation of the Mexican writer Alberto Ruy Sánchez's novel *Los jardines secretos de Mogador: Voices of the Earth* (2009). She also translated his novel *Poetics of Wonder: Passage to Mogador* (2014). She has translated works by the following Argentine authors: Mempo Giardinelli (*Bruno Fólner's Last Tango*, 2020); Tununa Mercado (*Chamber Canon*, 2022); Ana María Shua (*Quick Fix: Sudden Fiction*, 2008); and Perla Suez (*The Entre Ríos Trilogy*, 2006 and 2022; *Dreaming of the Delta*, 2014; and *The Devil's Country*, 2019.) For more information, please visit: www.rhondadahlbuchanan.com.